Touched by Sound

A Drummer's Journey

by

John Wyre

Drawings by Don Cooper

Buka Music
Norland, Ontario, Canada

TOUCHED BY SOUND
A Drummer's Journey
by John Wyre

Drawings by Don Cooper
Edited and designed by Jean Donelson

Buka Music
P.O. Box 100
Norland, Ontario
Canada K0M 2L0
E-mail: jdonwyre@peterboro.net

Copyright © 2002 by John Wyre

National Library of Canada Cataloguing in Publication Data

Wyre, John, 1941 -
   Touched by sound

    Includes bibliographical references.
    ISBN: 0-9730342-0-3

    1. Wyre, John, 1941 -   2. Drummers (Musicians)--Canada--Biography.   I. Title.

ML419.W97A3   2002   786.9'092   C2002-910208-1

Let the beauty we love—be what we do

—JELALUDDIN RUMI

PREFACE

In 1998 I did a master class on Playing Timpani in the Symphony Orchestra for students at Ithaca College in New York State. After the class several of the students approached me and told me I should write a book on the ideas I'd shared with them about music and sound.

My spiritual life is inexorably linked to music. Singing in the boys choir in church was my first experience of the joy of music. When my voice changed I was really upset. The search for a new voice led to the drum and gradually to the whole family of percussion instruments and a lifetime on the beaten path.

Sound has always been at the very core of my being. The use of sounds, music, and movement in the great spiritual traditions of the world has enriched the culture of humanity. This book explores how sound has woven such an influential path in the fabric of my life.

For Edna, 1910–2001
For Ross, 1906–1977

Where it all began

The pulse I felt as an embryo,
    my mother's heart,
the heaving waves of breathing,
    the vibrations the growing fetus feels,
the music my mother listened to—
    the great harpist Carlos Salzedo,
    the Philadelphia Orchestra—
the rhythm of her work,
the experience of birth,
all part of my being.

Our womb experience, from the moment of conception to the moment of our birth, plays a major role in shaping us physically, emotionally, and mentally.
—NAMGYAL RINPOCHE

PAYING ATTENTION

"Stop—Look—Listen"

It has taken me many years to realize the significance of this first lesson, which I learned my first day at school. Initially: how to cross the street without getting wasted by a car or truck; consequently, how to base your actions on what is really happening.

My greatest challenge in school, as in life, was paying attention. My dream department was active, and I found that I could lose myself in sounds—a process life has taught me to cherish. I was enchanted by pigeons cooing on the window sill, steam coming through the radiator pipes, the rhythm of the chalk on the blackboard, the tapping rhythms on desks and books, and other sounds that found their way into the classroom.

It was not long until the creation of my first musical instrument. At the time I had no name for it, but in retrospect it was a very simple form of *mbira*, an instrument common to many cultures in Africa that has evolved into a very sophisticated and sublime tradition among the Shona people of Zimbabwe. The recipe for my classroom mbira was simple: beg, borrow, or steal assorted hairpins from the girls sitting around you, remove the rubber tips, open the hairpins into a right angle and bend one half into another right angle—à la dogleg—and push the long end of the hairpins into a crack in the desk. Put all the hairpins into the crack about one-half inch apart and tune by pushing or pulling the long end of the pin farther in or out of the crack. Bass lines could be added by placing a ruler flat on the desk with the end of the ruler extended out over the edge of the desk by at least one-half its length—Voila! My first school ensemble.

My classmates' reaction to my first tool of annoyance ranged from joy and interaction to laughter or the silence of embarrassment. Most of the performances happened when the teacher was out of the room, but occasionally the instrument came in handy for punctuating and accompanying the events of the day, maybe an early attempt to escape from the cage of lessons that were part of school. Needless to say I drew the wrath of several teachers with this pastime.

Throughout my school years, including university, professors continued to remind me to join the class and pay attention. It took me a long time to realize that life is the real School and every day is filled with lessons. All we have to do to attend is pay attention. Simple—All Here and Now. Our tools are our natural intelligence, curiosity, and imagination—and hopefully they will lead us to a life of insight and new horizons.

Genetically, I was armed with my mother's take-charge stoic stubbornness (a Swiss characteristic) that established within me a need to do things my own way, to find and use my own solutions to the questions and opportunities in life. My father's positive artistic temperament gave me my strong dream department.

My mother, Edna Sprunger Wyre, was a nurse. Her leadership and people skills were very much a part of her work, and she became the director of nursing at the Frankford Hospital in Philadelphia.

My father, Ross, was a very special man, a fine musician, a great teacher, and a humanist who found something good in everyone. He was first and foremost a musician whose love for music was an inspiration. He played with the Philadelphia Orchestra, the Cincinnati Opera, Paul Whiteman, and many others. In 1935 the Philadelphia Board of Education asked him and violinist Mier Levin to develop a program for talented, serious students of music. This program was established at the Mastbaum Vocational Technical High School in Philadelphia. Gifted students from grades nine through twelve, and some veterans returning from military service, worked together four hours a day to develop their musical skills.

Dad never encouraged me to go into music. He understood that the need to pursue this path had to come from within me. When he realized that I was committed to music he was one-hundred percent behind my dreams. My parents' gifts to me are beyond words.

Having both parents working gave me a great deal of freedom to be me. My older sister, Rebecca (bless her sweet heart), and I grew up in a family that was filled with love. The constant nurturing spirit in our home was very much a part of the confidence that I felt as a child. I never ever observed a bad vibe between my parents. At first I thought all families were like mine. What a rude awakening I was in for. When I left home to go to university I was so innocent and idealistic about love that I was cruisin' for a bruisin'. Brief marriages changed my ideas of relationship, and my dad's advice—"If you're going to do something, do it till you get it right"—eventually proved to be helpful...

In 1974, I knocked on a door, and it opened to reveal a beautiful lady. The most instantaneous intuitive knowing consumed my being: that this was my partner, friend–lover–wife—to become the source of balance. Jean Donelson entered my life in an instant and has been guiding me through Love's Labyrinthine Garden ever since. We can work together and play together, yet we allow each other solitude and the freedom to pursue individual dreams.

As we sail this infinite sea of mystery
    on the raft of wonder
        the sails are made of curiosity
           the rudder—imagination
             the energy—love
                the voyage—transformation

BELLING

My first orgy of sound took place in the rural community of Kidron, Ohio, during the summer of 1948. My cousin Marge and her true love, Kenny, had recently tied the knot, and this particular evening they had settled down for a nice quiet night at home together. The entire community gathered, quite surreptitiously as was the custom of the "belling" tradition, and surrounded Marge and Kenny's home with the most unbelievable collection of sounds I had ever heard. As this was a community of Swiss immigrants, there were lots of beautiful bells—all sorts of cow bells, harness bells, carriage bells, hand bells, fire bells, and even large church bells that were mounted in the back of pickup trucks. There were huge saw blades from the lumber mill, suspended and struck with heavy hammers, anvils from the blacksmith, a women's chorus of pots and pans, rifles, pistols, firecrackers, and every imaginable variety of car and truck horn, all in place for the surprise serenade. The downbeat was given, and a celebration in sound that changed my life began, and it still resonates within me.

Cacophony or epiphany. The ear of the beholder comes in to play—hear. I approached this experience with the abandon and innocence of a seven-year-old. In retrospect, the natural musician in me was challenged to make sense of all this sound. Finding some order or form or line in this community celebration was like a trip to a sonic amusement park. All the bells provided a constant melodic and harmonic interaction. The pots and pans and anvils were the rhythm section. The giant saw blades were the gongs and tam tams, adding unique textures, color, and harmony. The car, truck, and novelty horns were a delightful source of humor and surprise. All this served to support and set up the explosions from the guns and firecrackers that danced atop the entire ensemble. The spontaneity of the event secured within me the validity of improvisation as a source of vitality and sincere expression. What a liberating force!

Crashing pot lids together, I wandered around the outside of the house interacting with the soundscape that had exploded in this quiet farming community. The whole town was engaged in total abandon, a joyous dance of vibrations recognizing and celebrating the union of love and marriage. A "belling" is usually the overture to a party, so the cacophonous serenade continued until Marge and Kenny emerged from their house and showed their appreciation by feeding the entire gathering.

GUIDES

We learn by doing.
Undertaking brings blessing.

Guides are beings, experiences, or things that encourage action. Guides can be teachers, preachers, friends, lovers, letters, words, the songs of birds; winos, students, partners, farmers, charmers, trees, bees, frogs, flowers, stones, bones; cats, dogs, and hollowed-out logs. Anything can be a guide. Guides are unpredictable; you never know when they will appear, but when they do it's always a strong experience. They motivate, inspire productivity, remove mental obstacles, and move us to do what we know we have to do—some day I'll heed my own advice 'cause it's been clear all my life—they remind us that we can, and we love them. Sometimes they just smile and we see.

Guides
Every musician I've danced with along this path of sound
The touch of Love
Unison—union—shared devotion
Family
Cultural enchantment—every land I've lived
Cities—Communities
Music—The Sound of the Spirit

Quiet hall—to sit and call the silence—that's all
The Sound of the Space
Cathedrals—Temples—Concert Halls—Homes—
Forest—Garden

Space has a spiritual equivalent and can heal what is divided and burdensome in us.

—Gretel Ehrlich

All Guides

The great mentors in my life—those people who have been able to reach out and touch me, to motivate me to work, to inspire me to respond to my life experience in a productive way—have all reached me with the power of their personal example.

Music was always an important part of my life. There was always music at home. Growing up in Philadelphia was a musical bonanza. Due to the vision and persuasive character of Dr. Louis G. Wersen, the educational system in the public schools had made a major commitment to music. I made the journey from piano to trumpet to clarinet, searching for an instrument that would say yes to me.

One day, at an assembly in my elementary school, an orchestra was playing. A young Kalman Cherry demonstrated the timpani, and I was converted to the art of touching. Kalman was the first timpanist who really turned me on, set my imagination aflame, and started me along the beaten path. I am grateful to Kalman for his artistry and friendship. At the age of twelve I had found my instrument, and I began lessons with Fred D. Hinger who at that time was the timpanist with the Philadelphia Orchestra.

Fred Daniel Hinger
A great master of touch

He touched me with his understanding of sound production, expanding my palette of colors and enriching the language of percussion.

He touched me with his insatiable curiosity that created a need within him to make everything better.

He touched me with his artistry—sensitive, powerful, and always the servant of the music.

I started studying with Dan Hinger in 1954 and stayed in touch with him until I said good-bye to him at his memorial service on January 15, 2001.

I feel so fortunate to have been able to share so many years with this extraordinary man, whose example and teaching laid the foundation and instilled the positive energy within me to support my own explorations of sound through the art of touching.

Dan showed me the importance of one note. His enthusiastic response to the sound of one touch was an explosion of well-being and positive reinforcing energy. He thoroughly understood how our energy and touch combine to influence the character of the sound we produce. His curiosity and craftsmanship combined to create new instruments and mallets, and it was a great lesson for me to observe the evolution of his perceptions and how he integrated them into the sound of the Philadelphia Orchestra—and what a sound it was!

Lessons with Dan were always filled with his powerful enthusiasm for his art and a consistent sense of joy in making music. As well as the exploration of the world of percussion, every lesson with Dan would open you to whatever was fascinating his imagination. Often he shared with me his love of wildlife through his interest in bird watching. Archery was another of the interests he shared with me. And I remember a lesson in which he also taught me to adjust the brakes on his Volkswagen Beetle!

One of my strongest memories of lessons with Dan was hearing him asking me if I understood, and realizing that I hadn't been listening to him. This probably inspired him to introduce me to *Zen and the Art of Archery*; I think he sensed that my major challenge in life would be to learn to pay attention and concentrate.

Dan was not a teacher to turn out clones. His confidence was that of a very centered and extremely powerful person, and he was very skilled at instilling this confidence in his students, teaching them to explore and to use their instruments as a playground for their imagination.

Dan's influence on Bill Cahn, Russell Hartenberger, and myself has made him a major part of Nexus. He encouraged us to pursue our dreams, and indeed we have.

I remember most his generosity, his wonderful nurturing spirit, and his supreme confidence.

A very precious spirit sings on in all those who were fortunate enough to share in his life.

❖

A good teacher will lead you within. Don't be a clone, the only real path is your own. Eventually we come to see that the wages of existence are to be nurturing, to develop an active love for all life forms. To embrace the organic wholeness of the Universe—to love that and know that this Great Mystery that we are part of—is infinite.

❖

In the 1950s the music program in the public schools of Philadelphia was such that any student, from elementary through senior high, who was serious about music could be excused from regular classes to observe specific rehearsals of the Philadelphia Orchestra. This sublime ensemble was nurtured by a rich history of collaborations among great artists, including the legendary Leopold Stokowski, an artist whose vision was clearly anchored in the exploration of sound. Stokowski changed the traditional set-up of the orchestra. He experimented with transcriptions and reorchestration and embraced free bowing in the string sections in pursuit of his vision.

Another key factor in the sound of the orchestra was its home, the Academy of Music. Great orchestras do not exist without the benevolence of a positive acoustical environment in which to rehearse and perform. The old Academy was opened in 1857 and acclaimed as one of America's first great opera houses. It has been a major influence on the sound of the orchestra. I remember sitting way up in the amphitheater in the quiet hall before concerts, listening to some of the musicians, including the timpanist (my teacher, Dan Hinger), warm up. If there was not too much activity on stage it was possible to have a conversation with Dan without either one of us having to raise our voices above a normal talking level, an exquisite acoustical phenomenon. Contemporary renovations to the Academy, necessary due to deterioration and changes in building codes, did not help the sound of the orchestra. There has been positive reponse to the recent opening of the Kimmel Center for the Performing Arts, and the orchestra's new home, Verizon Hall. This confirms the confidence of the Board of the orchestra in hiring Russell Johnson and his colleagues at Artec to look after the acoustical concerns of the new hall. Obviously there needs to be a period of adjustment, while the Artec people tune their work and the musicians make their adjustments to this new sound environment. Within a few seasons, we will have a much clearer idea of the success of this marriage between this great orchestra and its new home.

I have experienced many of the great concert halls in the world, and among the contemporary concert venues that were built in the second half of the twentieth century, Russell Johnson's work stands out, demonstrating his genius at creating magnificent acoustical environments.

The first large orchestra I played in was the All-Philadelphia Senior High School Orchestra, and I remember my first buzz in 1956 playing Chabrier's "España" and Dvorak's Symphony in D Minor. I was enchanted, and was transported into a world that for me is still filled with wonder and inspiration.

Michael Bookspan, a percussionist in the Philadelphia Orchestra, used to visit the percussion section to tutor us, and his insights were a great motivation for me. His approach was very natural. He was a great help in simplifying the technical questions we had, and he was skilled at instilling confidence to meet the demands of the performances. In one session I was finding it difficult to produce soft cymbal crashes. Bringing the cymbals together in a consistent way was not working for me. Mickey suggested starting the stroke with the cymbals together—success!

Mickey's courage and integrity touched me deeply, and to this day I cherish our friendship. Mickey's example said: Go for it!—be real—live it—don't just think about it. Don't just talk about it. Get to work and live with the courage of your convictions. A life of action finds satisfaction.

In my youth I was always drawn to nature and wanted very much to be a farmer. In eighth grade I went to visit the Wissahickon Farm School to see what it was about. The school was situated in Fairmount Park in Philadelphia. In grades nine through twelve the students majored in the many aspects of agriculture. The only thing missing that I was interested in was music. So I decided to follow the normal academic course, doing my ninth grade of junior high and shifting my dream of being a farmer to one of pursuing veterinary science, following the path of my grandfather and my uncle, which would allow me to access music programs as I prepared for university.

Ninth grade provided many new challenges. This final year in junior high school was in a different and much tougher neighborhood. The fighting and violence in and around the school often brought the police to calm the tensions of gang fights and personal confrontations. Young male hormones, social injustices, and adolescent frustrations were raging in this environment. Music became a refuge for me, a place where I could escape the violence of the street. I discovered that by becoming a musician I established a character within the social structure of the school that was respected, and this gave me confidence and strength to meet these new challenges.

Once I entered high school I started playing drum set in rock 'n' roll and jazz groups, and pop music along the Jersey shore on summertime road trips. I listened to Ed Thigpen on drum set. His music always moved me, touching me in a very real way. I listened—and loved to play.

Eastman School of Music

So, my dream in high school had been to be a veterinarian, but when the time came to go to university I found it impossible to leave music behind. The new dream was to be timpanist in a symphony orchestra. I entered the Eastman School of Music in Rochester, New York, in 1959, to study with William Street. A wonderful gentleman and a sensitive artist, Bill Street showed me about playing from the heart. He had shared most of his musical journey with his brother Stanley, until Stan became ill and had to retire from performance. In lessons, Bill would often wander through his memories, walk to the marimba, pick up a pair of mallets, play through some of the tunes he used to do with his brother, and make me cry. Then we'd sit and light up a couple of cigars and I would listen to Bill talk about the good old days of playing in the pit for vaudeville and movies, and the early days of the Rochester Philharmonic.

Along with William Street, the Eastman School of Music was loaded with Guides. Frederick Fennell taught me to Be Prepared to play my part and to Listen! Listen! Listen! Maestro Fennell shared his joy, like a kid with a toy, and every time he did his dance the music came to life. He inspired us to love what we do.

Francis Tursi brought the wisdom of a sage to his performance and teaching of the viola. He opened my mind to the idea of visualization (hear the sound before you play) and advised me to explore the cultures of Asia.

All percussionists collect sounds. In the 1960s I began collecting instruments from many different cultures. My first assignment from John Galm, my Big Brother at Eastman, was to go to the music library, take out a recording of a gamelan orchestra from Indonesia and listen to it. I will love John forever for opening that door, and for showing me that there was an extraordinary wealth of music in the family of humanity. In 1959 he told me to get myself a ticket to hear Ravi Shankar, then on his first North American tour, and it was at that concert that I first heard a master of the North Indian tabla, Chatur Lal. My imagination was set afire and I was mesmerized by a whole new world of music. In 1962 I was blown away by Babatunde Olatunji, Nigeria's musical ambassador. He was the first African musician I had ever heard. Thus began for me a dialogue with a continent that is one of the cultural treasure houses of the world.

Marlboro Music Festival

One of the great blessings in my life has been my participation at the Marlboro Music Festival in the Green Mountains of Vermont. Founded in 1951 by Adolf Busch, his brother Herman, Rudolf Serkin, and Marcel, Blanche and Louis Moyse, Marlboro truly marries the benevolence and inspiration of the natural environment of the Green Mountains with making music in a joyous, loving way. Marlboro is a gathering of artists who share a lifetime commitment to the magic and majesty of sound; a family of equals exploring their dreams and ideas about music through the most selfless community of musical spirits I have ever experienced.

My initial observation of Becoming One—losing the self in the music—came while playing timpani in the Marlboro Festival Orchestra in 1961, with Pablo Casals conducting. Every musician on stage had so much love and respect for the great maestro. These virtuoso artists were pouring their hearts out for the master and the music, creating a paradise for this young timpanist, and I realized that I had reached a new state, one that was not self-projected.

Casals was in his eighties then. He liked to sit backstage in a large comfortable chair during the rehearsal breaks, with his ever-present pipe in his right hand and an oxygen mask in the other. What a study in balance.

The experiences of eight summers at Marlboro and the all-important guides I found there could fill a book:

Rudolph Serkin—his vision and the inspirational force of his character were the foundation of the festival. The example of his Meditative Meandering around the concert hall and back stage in Preparation for performance was a wonderful lesson for me. The ordinariness of this extraordinary artist was a tutorial in humility. I'll never forget the musical paradise that was created at an informal concert when Serkin accompanied Benita Valente and Maureen Forrester as they sang together.

Marcel Moyse showed me tone development through interpretation—color, intensity, line. His wind classes at Marlboro were the ultimate university of expression.

Karen Tuttle taught me to relax—completely—all the way. Read the body language; use the whole body.

Harold 'Buddy' Wright, whose artistry was a powerful force in the Boston Symphony, made every phrase a mystical journey.

Julie Levine—Love every note you play.

Mike Bloom—Go for it! One hundred percent.

Michael Rabin—an effortless musician who communicated through the music from his violin what he could not articulate with words.

Ornulf Gulbransen—No limits to human expression. Living proof that only the young have youth, but only the old know how to use it.

Mischa Schneider was the cellist in the Budapest Quartet for over forty years, and his wealth of experience, both artistic and human, was profound. The quality of his pizzicato on his Gofrillier cello inspired me to explore the timpani in search of new sounds. Along with his insights into the human condition came a list of restaurants in which to eat in Europe, drawn from forty years on the road.

Mischa was a keen observer of life. During the summer of 1963, Zoltan Kodaly came to Marlboro, and at one evening performance I witnessed Leslie Parnas's performance of Kodaly's Unaccompanied Sonata for Cello. Leslie is a musician of great gifts, capable of capturing your heart and seducing you with the magic of his performance. I was moved by the experience and felt that the sonata was very special. As so often happened at Marlboro, my imagination became consumed by new experience, and I wandered about singing phrases from the latest tune that had captured my attention, this time from Kodaly's sonata.

One day Mischa asked if I would come to fetch him following a meeting with Casals. I was delighted not only for the opportunity to spend some time with Mischa but for the opportunity to observe a dialogue between these two great men. When I arrived at the farm where Casals was living, his wife, Marta, showed me into the room where the two masters were involved in their conversation. Eventually their dialogue came upon the sonata that had so captured my imagination a few nights before, and Casals said to Mischa, "I was talking to Kodaly, and I said to him, 'In your sonata, you have written everything that is possible to write for the cello, but tell me, where is the music?' " This comment struck me like a dagger to the heart. The great man had just severely challenged my understanding...and it hurt.

As I drove out the driveway I turned to Mischa and asked for help. I told him how much I loved the Kodaly sonata and how dumb struck I was at Casals's comments. He smiled and said, "John, you are going to meet many extraordinary people in your life. Always take what is good, take what is positive, and leave everything else behind."

We all have our limitations. Having a genetic predisposition to optimism it's easy for me to say, "Avoid the dialogue of the negative." When we consider that every day we can add to life's joy or to life's pain, the choice seems obvious.

❖

Finding solutions—there are no limitations to the self except those you believe in. Belief is merely doubt dressed up. Belief and habit dull the mind.

Nothing is to be feared—only understood.

❖

At Marlboro in 1968 we did a performance of *Les Noces* by Stravinsky. At the end of the first rehearsal, on stage in the empty hall, I found myself hanging out with Bill Cahn, Bob Becker, Robin Engelman and Russell Hartenberger. We were all young percussionists at the time, and in the process of joking around each of us approached the xylophone and played our versions of the xylophone part from *Porgy and Bess*, one of the more difficult excerpts in the orchestral xylophone repertoire. Bob "Dr. Wizard" Becker walked up to the xylophone after the rest of us had finished our renditions and played the thing in octaves! It was quite clear who the virtuoso was.

After leaving Eastman in 1964, I spent one season as timpanist of the Oklahoma City Symphony. In Oklahoma I met K. Dean Walker, a fine musician and the first woman to hold the position of principal percussionist in a symphony orchestra in North America. K. Dean was full of the joy of making music and encouraged me greatly, helping guide me through my first season in a professional orchestra.

With hindsight it is now interesting and heartening to observe the evolution of the participation of women in the professional world of music performance over the last forty years.

The other angel I met in Oklahoma City was a mockingbird whose stage was the telephone pole outside my bedroom window. Every morning I would linger on the mattress completely seduced by the vast repertoire, the expressive range, and the sincerity of the mockingbird.

❖

> The bird does not sing because it has an answer,
> it sings because it has a song.
>
> —TRAD. CHINESE

❖

In 1965 I left Oklahoma City and assumed the position of timpanist in the Milwaukee Symphony. Here a huge lesson awaited me about the need for discipline and restraint in the face of frustration.

With my youthful impatience and idealism I had been gathering and storing frustrating experiences during the entire symphony season. Towards the end of a school concert, circumstances conspired to put me over the edge.

The conductor was in the habit of announcing to the student audience what music we were about to perform, without announcing it to the musicians in the orchestra. He would turn quickly, giving the downbeat, and only the strings in the front of the orchestra, who could hear the conductor's choice, knew what to play, so the rest of us could not enter until we recognized the tune and had frantically searched for the music in our folders.

Well, one afternoon I could stand no more, and instead of scrambling for my music to Smetana's "The Bartered Bride" I reacted by beginning to improvise. The overture became a timpani concerto. I lost it completely, banging away in frustration and drowning out the orchestra. The energy was unbelievable, but what I played had little to do with the music, at least as Smetana had imagined it.

After the concert the orchestra committee called an emergency meeting to discuss my behavior. Some committee members were calling for my dismissal, others were still laughing, when the personnel manager, Fred Clem, stood up and said, "He only did what we've all wanted to do." Meeting adjourned. Nevertheless, the next day I flew to Toronto to audition for a new job.

So, in 1966 I settled in Toronto as timpanist of the Toronto Symphony, where I fell in love with the city, the orchestra, and its young maestro, Seiji Ozawa, whose humility, sincerity, vitality, and spontaneity taught me so much, and whose generosity and friendship introduced me to the extraordinary culture of Japan. Seiji also opened my life and heart to Toru Takemitsu.

The Toronto Symphony became my orchestral family. Over the fifteen years from 1966 to 1981 I was timpanist for eleven seasons. Karel Ancerl followed Seiji's tenure and brought the wisdom, craftsmanship and discipline of a seasoned master.

One day in rehearsal a musician tried to make excuses for his shortcoming by explaining his profound understanding of the music in question; Maestro Ancerl's response: "Don't believe everything you think."

A state of mind can make us blind. Often we suffer from acute astuteness or defensive knowingness.

❖

Don't be kidnapped by preferences; it will only lead to paralysis by analysis.

❖

Let Be What Is.

❖

I left the Toronto Symphony in 1970 after my first four seasons. I began composing, then wandered in Asia, and enjoyed a change from the regular routine of orchestral discipline. After a brief return to the TSO, I spent 1972 to 1975 building a home, composing, exploring nature, teaching at the University of Toronto's Faculty of Music, and doing several tours with the San Francisco Symphony.

From 1975 to 1981 I was back in the TSO family, working with the orchestra's new director, Andrew Davis, a genius with the large choral works; he brought young energy, a brilliant sense of ensemble, and adventuresome programming to the TSO. I fell in love again with Judy Loman, who is blessed with the gift of making every note she plays on her harp irresistible. She was the song bird of the orchestra for more than forty years. And Big Sam Davis, who loved to play the bass—with joy in every note. And Eugene Rittich, principal horn, who could take you on the most marvelous journeys with his long musical line. They were just a few of the many wonderful musicians in the Toronto Symphony family who inspired me with their music.

Don Wherry, one of my colleagues in the percussion section of the TSO, was a very open and generous person who loved to share his sense of exploration—a gift that ultimately led to his establishing and directing the Sound Symposium in St. John's, Newfoundland.

Don and I shared a large closet in the old home of the TSO, Massey Hall. We used this closet space for storing instruments and concert dress, leaving just enough room for changing into performance attire, or just hangin' out. Often after concerts we would unwind in this room by improvising with the most unusual combinations of sounds, occasionally inviting a guest to sit in. During my student days at Eastman I had established the process of suspending instruments (bells, drums, cymbals, gongs, etc.) from the ceiling, so Don and I did this, and our Massey Hall closet became a maze of sounds, often requiring extensive reconnoitering in order to move around or change clothes. Eventually the whole space evolved into a giant kinetic sculpture that we interacted with whenever we were in the room. Often we set surprises for each other by rearranging everything to create an entirely new soundscape, rigging lines to the door that would release a barrage of sound when anyone entered the room.

One evening I approached the door to prepare for the evening's concert, being careful as usual. I opened the door very slowly, decided there were no strings attached, then opened the door wide. Satisfied that a stack of cymbals would not rain down on me, I reached in, turned on the light switch, and all hell broke loose. Don had gone high tech on me by wiring an old radio to the light switch, tuning the radio to a heavy rock station, and turning up the volume!

This room of surprises was always filled with a delightful spontaneity. I missed Don when he left the orchestra in 1972 to pursue his dreams in Newfoundland. His sudden passing in the summer of 2001 was a great loss. His vision and his generosity changed the cultural landscape of St. John's, and his spirit left an indelible mark on the creative community there.

> Change is ceaseless, and the opportunity for
> transformation is NOW.

Change—The Constant Condition

It is part of the human condition to:
    Observe, Absorb, Ponder, and Transform.

Transformation

We cannot advance without leaving things behind.
It's not a sacrifice, it's the wage of freedom.
Are we willing to give up what we have so as
    to be what we are not?

All this flies in the face of a desire for permanence, security, predictability, rules, authority, control, plans, and consistency, constantly challenging our idea of what should be.

In the 1960s and 1970s I found myself being an orchestral timpanist, a chamber music festival participant, a collector of instruments and musics of other cultures, a coach for the young percussionists of the National Youth Orchestra of Canada, and being actively involved in New Music Concerts in Toronto. I was also playing in the Canadian Opera Company orchestra and doing occasional studio work in Toronto. An amazing diversity of performance opportunities and musical styles. The contemporary music scene was blossoming, especially for percussion.

Improvisation

Answering a knock on the door, I met Michael Craden. He introduced himself, brought greetings from Emil Richards in Hollywood, and we proceeded to my basement music room. Here, of course, were suspended bells, gongs and cymbals, as well as drums of all sizes and shapes from a variety of cultures, homemade instruments of wood, metallophones constructed from different types of metal tubing, shakers, scrapers, and a collection of found objects (brake drums, metal springs, slinkys, pot lids) that were simply beautiful sounds.

Michael and I began to improvise. The lighting in the basement was very subdued, almost non-existent, as we listened our way around the room. I was playing very softly, fading in and out of what Michael was doing, trying to listen and accompany him. Suddenly he stopped, turned to me and shouted, "Hey man! If you're going to play with me you've got to mean it!!!" One of the greatest performance lessons of my life. Michael and I became fast friends.

Michael was one of the founding members of Nexus. His improvisational skills were magical. He found places to play that were unimaginable, charming, and challenging, on his way to new horizons in spontaneity.

A simple fascination with sound has sustained and developed my enthusiasm for improvisation. Through all the passions and obsessions of collecting sounds and building new instruments in response to the influence of the ear, improvisation has provided me with a means to bring these sounds to life in the form of music. Years ago I remember watching the Flip Wilson Show on TV. His guest was Erroll Garner, and after a sublime journey on the piano under the guidance of Garner's amazing improvisational skills, Flip Wilson approached the great musician and asked him if he ever played a wrong note. Erroll Garner looked up from the piano, smiled and said. "There are no wrong notes. If something sounds strange to you, just listen to it for awhile and it will sound fine."

Another thought that was influential in freeing me from the prison of my own concepts came from composer R. Murray

Schafer. In his work with young people in a program he called "The Composer in the Classroom" Murray presented the idea that

"Melody is like taking a walk with a note."

I was free to just wander through all the impressions that appeared in the ears as I danced from sound to sound.

In my late twenties the idea grew within me that if I was a musician I should be able to walk out on stage and make music spontaneously. No printed charts, no tunes memorized, no habit patterns, just a spontaneous reaction to the sounds as they unfolded. Considering the fact that by that period in my life I had collected so many instruments from many different cultures and had constructed many new instruments of my own design, improvisation seemed to be a logical way of exploring all of these new (to me) sounds and expanding the colors of my musical palette.

Improvisation led me to interesting collaborations in both film and live theater. In 1983 Patrick Watson came to my home, along with director John McGreevy, to explore a theater production of the Old Testament classic, The Book of Job. Patrick, never one to rest on his many laurels, had memorized the entire Book of Job, and we proceeded to develop the dialogue of words and characters and sounds that led to productions at Toronto's Nathan Cohen Studio in December 1983, then at the National Arts Centre in Ottawa in March 1984. I shared the stage with Patrick, responding spontaneously with my instruments to his interpretation of the strong story of humanity's understanding of despair and its place in the universe. One of Canada's most productive visionaries, Patrick Watson remains a profound motivational source in my life.

Another Patrick who has had a strong influence in my life is Patrick Spence-Thomas. He is imbued with an inordinate dose of enthusiasm and joy that he brings to his love of recording and film technology. Patrick's generosity and expertise is legendary among those who have had the good fortune to work with him. I recall a collaboration with film director Paul Almond in Patrick's Toronto studio on Jarvis Street. Robin Engelman and I had our instruments set up and Paul would assume a fetal position, knees and forehead touching the floor. From this posture he would build his being into a primal scream of emotional and descriptive dialogue à la cosmic preacher, setting a specific mood, and then returning to his fetal stillness while Robin and I responded, trying to capture Paul's mood in sound. Not your ordinary film session.

This need to experience an improvisational approach to music and the exploration of the sounds we had collected from around the world led to the formation of, and became the roots of, NEXUS: Bob Becker, Bill Cahn, Michael Craden, Robin Engelman, Russell Hartenberger, and myself. Nexus has been improvising together now for over thirty years, each musician bringing his perceptions and character to the process of making music spontaneously.

Confirmation of the improvisatory approach to film scores came in a project with Larry Crosley, a composer who had done many projects for Crawley Films. Budge Crawley had purchased some Japanese footage shot in the Himalayas, documenting Yuichiro Miura's attempt to ski down Mt. Everest. The footage was stunning, and Crosley approached me to see if Nexus could be involved in his score for the film. I suggested to Crosley that he consider bringing Bob Aitken, the incredible flutist, together with Nexus and have us improvise to the film.

He decided to try this. We filled the studio at Manta Sound in Toronto with our instruments, and Dave Green, the engineer, established the sound balances. The movie was screened directly into the studio. Crosley had determined where he wanted music and before each cue he would describe the scene and set the mood, then we played to picture. We worked for two days with no contract, no agreement on fees except the guarantee that if they were not happy with what we created we would return and play whatever score Crosley put together.

The sessions were amazing, and when we finished Budge Crawley and his producer came into the studio from the control booth, dancing in ecstasy, and we completed our negotiations in short order. The film, "The Man Who Skied Down Everest," went on to win an Academy Award for Best Documentary of 1975. It confirmed the value of working in an improvisatory way and trusting the creative instincts of the musicians.

❖

We learn to speak by speaking, to study by studying, to run by running, to work by working; in just the same way, we learn to love by loving.

—Saint Francis de Sales

❖

We learn to improvise by improvising.

NEXUS

Six very different characters
Bob Becker – Bill Cahn – Michael Craden –
Robin Engelman – Russell Hartenberger – John Wyre

In 1971, through a variety of professional and personal friendships, the ensemble NEXUS was formed. Our first concert was organized by the composer Warren Benson. Warren is an amazing creative spirit whose encouragement and motivation made him the midwife at the birth of Nexus.

This first Nexus concert took place in Kilbourn Hall at the Eastman School of Music on May 22, 1971. We filled the stage with instruments and improvised, exploring our way through the entire concert.

Never in my wildest imaginings as a young player did I ever dream of spending a large part of my professional career on the road with a band of drummers. More than three decades later I think of Nexus with words like **family, trust,** and **sensitivity.** A powerful performance vehicle blended with endearing friendships, Nexus is over thirty years of making music together, exploring the world together, sharing the stage from individual spontaneity to exquisite ensemble precision. Sharing life, from the extraordinary challenges of skill and will, to the benevolence of the intuitive knowing. Nexus has generated a sanctuary for the creative spirit—a brotherhood based on the freedom to be what we are.

Bob—His genius for complexity, his discipline, hard work, and a sense of perfection that transcends the limitations the human condition usually imposes, have made him a legend in the profession as one of the great virtuosos of our time. Speaking of time, Bob's sense of it all is so magical and full of vitality that every music he touches comes to life in such a powerful way that it makes you want to dance. A composer's dream come true, every note you write sounds much better than what you imagined because of Bob's magic. Being thorough in thought can make him distraught or slow to react to this or that fact. Bob is living proof that hard work is rewarded with extraordinary results. His sound is bright and precise, and his rhythm is hot and on top.

Bill—The joy of his performance is palpable. His imagination is free and soaring, like a cross between a child and a bird. Overflowing with spontaneity and enthusiasm, Bill can always be counted on to be outstanding in the way he communicates and surprises. He's living proof that there is no accounting for taste. Bill deals with the stresses of life with a wonderful sense of humor, and when he cracks himself up he loses it completely. If laughter is the best medicine, then we should call him Dr. Cahn. His cahncepts, cahnfusion, cahnstructions, cahntracts, cahnducting, cahntradictions, and cahnjecture have all led to enchanting cahnsequences. Bill's sound and rhythm are both a joyful and a restless dance, wandering imaginatively and all-ways in relation to what's happening in the music. Bill's business and administrative skills, along with a selfless commitment to the Nexus family, carried us through the 1990s and brought us through the challenges of contracts, organizing tours, and coordinating the work of all our agents around the world.

Michael had great visual gifts. His paintings, drawings, and sculptures were a major part of his all-too-short life. His music was overflowing with spontaneity and sincerity. Like Bill he had a marvelous sense of humor and timing, and the dialogue between the two of them often had us in a joyful fit of laughter as we ran out on stage to perform. Michael was an artist. He had no choice. He didn't read music and considered notation "fly shit." It simply got in the way. Michael's creative energy was a powerful force in Nexus until his untimely death from cancer in 1982, and his spirit remains with us to this day. Michael's gift to Nexus was establishing the tradition of responding to the music at any time, in any way, anywhere, with anything—Freedom to Be—Nexus is living proof that Michael's melody lingers on.

Robin brings enormous authority to his performance and to his life. Robin and I have been making music together since 1965 when we met in the Milwaukee Symphony. We've shared it all from the sublime to the absurd. From ecstasy to the furies of frustration, we found our unison in music's meliorative miracle. Fearless in the face of injustice, Robin would not tolerate the abuse of his orchestra colleagues by conductors, and he would respond decisively to defend their human dignity. No person has ever challenged me more than Robin. He's living proof that pain is growth. Robin and I perceive, think, and live in very different ways, and often our dialogue within Nexus is strong, providing an arena for the processing of ideas within the ensemble. Change and contradictions challenge his sense of authority, often leading to rehearsal rage (a form of excessive energy). With Robin I have experienced the wonderful way music adjusts and attunes differences. His sound is emphatic and his rhythm is determined.

Russell is living proof that those who know don't speak. He's a man of few words, but when he speaks—listen up! There's lots of wisdom there. Russ is the rock of Nexus. His music is so solid you can always hang your hat on it. In performance, whenever that lostness takes over and deposits you in limbo, and your whole being cries out, where the hell are we, you don't need a joker responding with "Des Moines!" All you have to do is listen to Russell and it's very clear where the music is. In the 1970s Russ and I did a radio show for Tim Wilson, a producer for the CBC. Tim had us both wired up to monitor our heartbeats. We had headphones on to hear the pulse of our pumps. While my heart was dancing all over the place, wandering from fast to slow like a bee looking for honey, Russell's heartbeat never wavered, steady like a mountain. Russell is very perceptive and has been ordained with a great deal of common sense—the least common of all senses. A peacemaker with a PhD in the music of the world, Russ is a wonderful teacher, a patient, nurturing spirit who has made my day so often in the past thirty years. His sound is solid and clear, and his rhythm is right there in the pocket.

John: I'm an optimist, a dreamer, passionate and undisciplined to a fault. Music seems to come from a super-sensual sacredness, a marriage of sound and motion that has always been part of my life. Born to play in my very own way and more interested in experiencing than understanding. My ego loves to lead, yet the musician in me loves to accompany. My sound is relaxed, my rhythm laid back. I've always been enchanted by sound and confident to go where it leads, accepting what's there and treating it with care. My neglect of technique makes my approach unique and often leaves me up the creek. Good fortune in the realization of many dreams has set me singing many themes.

Both Bill and I each had our turn at being the business manager for Nexus. Managing an ensemble of musicians in which you are a performing member presents many challenges, among them remaining friends with your colleagues. I opted for friendship and gave up the managing role following our four-month international tour in 1984. Bill did likewise in 1998 after ten years at the helm.

In our years together as an ensemble Nexus has tried many different approaches to organizing and managing all the varied aspects of our career. After all this time shared, we know each other so well that our business meetings often set new standards for dysfunctional, unproductive sessions of shoot the messenger and my idea can beat up your idea. Honesty is too painful, responses too predictable. Enter Ray Dillard to the Nexus family, functioning as a positive facilitator in Nexus meetings as well as managing our business affairs.

Ray is a very special character: a fine percussionist, a sensitive musician, a wizard with the technology of computers and the recording industry, and he possesses extraordinary people skills. He's produced most of our recordings and has a deep understanding of our music, our instruments, and our individual characters.

And thank you, Canada, for responding, for nurturing and supporting Nexus. The tolerance of differences, the social conscience, and the benevolent and cosmopolitan culture of Toronto inspired us to pursue our dreams and establish our home in that great city. All levels of government in Canada, through their Arts Councils, Foreign Affairs Department, and the Canadian Broadcasting Corporation (both Radio and Television), and the University of Toronto have all played major roles in our survival for the past three decades.

Nexus

Russell is the maypole
    Bill is the jester
Bob is the accelerator
    Robin the arrester
John is a dreamer
    Robin a screamer
Bob is a wizard
    Russell—a redeemer.

Bill is full of song
    Bob in thought—too long
Russell speaks so seldom
    Robin strong—but wrong
John is stubborn, can't be told
Robin's heart is made of gold —
    he'll turn your crank beyond the
    edge but never leave you in the cold.

Epic Head meets the Big Mac of thought.

Bill—like a child
    can never end his play
John—like a child
    who has to have his way
Robin's temper can't be missed
    especially when he's really pissed.

    Don't Touch Me!

Michael, your spirit's in our midst.

Bob is oh so serious
    practicing to be delirious
Russ was born mature—
    and born to play—I'm sure.

Nexus the creature
    trying to reach her
sometimes a preacher
    all ways a teacher.

We started out with trunks on backs
    and now we only talk by fax
then fly somewhere and share a meal
    and tell some jokes to relax the feel.

We realized that in sharing thoughts
    with ideas and words
    we would rarely agree
so we let our ears
    guide our careers
    and the music set us free.

This crazy band has roamed the land
    in search of who we are
by ship and boat, by train and plane
    by truck and jeep and car.
We've walked a lot and talked a lot
    and dreamed and screamed and played
and through it all we've had a ball
    all shared with friends we've made.

The world is vast and what a cast
    of colleagues we have found
of every size and shape and hue
    walking on the path of sound
from Fairbanks south to Adelaide
    the road has been our home
from Shanghai to Finlandia
    we still continue to roam.

Our music comes from where we've been
and who we've met and what we've found
amazing mix of pulse and line
    what magic . . . the miracle of sound.

What we are today we owe to each other

    Beautiful

❖

While they [Nexus] are in full possession of the astounding technique and professional bases implied in modern music, they perform simply for the joy of making music.

—Toru Takemitsu

❖

TORU TAKEMITSU

As a confident young musician who had graduated from a music school, I assumed that I knew what music was. In 1967 I had my first encounter with the composer Toru Takemitsu, and he would become one of the most profound mentors and guides in my life. By his benevolent example he showed me that I did not know what music was, and thus he converted my life to one of exploration.

When I began composing I started by drawing sound, inspired by the beautiful work of R. Murray Schafer. I was certain that I could render visually what the ears could imagine. When I asked Takemitsu about notation his words were simple and open: "Notation changes the noun music into the verb music." Toru could always find a positive spin on the questions of the moment and prompt you to face life in a more realistic way. He was skilled at bringing about a balance in one's view of the moment, or totally disarming your concerns with his sense of humor.

I remember a September afternoon in 1970. We had just finished the first rehearsal of my first composition, "Bells." The premiere was to take place in two days with the Japan Philharmonic. Lucas Foss was conducting and I was performing the solo percussion part. Toru, Lucas and I were sitting in the bar of the Tokyo Hilton Hotel. I was very depressed and Toru turned to Lucas, nodded toward me and said, "Virgin composer." I asked Toru if first rehearsals were always this bad. He laughed and said, "No, they get worse!"

Wandering through one of the many temple gardens in the Kyoto area: As always, Toru was sharing some of his favorite spaces and giving us an intimate experience with some of the most exquisite aspects of his culture. As we meandered along a path beside a pond our attention was seduced by a frog jumping into the water. We were all united in silence, observing the influence of the frog on the surface of the water, the ever-greater concentric circles ultimately kissing the earth at the far edge of the pond. Toru's gentle observation, "A little ripple goes a long way," reminds me to this day of the consequences of our actions.

In a conversation with Toru in 1976 during the first Nexus tour of Japan, we were discussing the challenges of managing a group of musicians, and I confessed my frustrations in trying to deal with some people. Toru's response was one of the great lessons of my life: "You must always remember that they are coming at you with a good heart." So forget the style, the veneer that confronts you. In order to heal the distance between those we disagree with, we must pursue a more intimate understanding of each other and learn to work together without friction.

Toru Takemitsu was born in 1930 and died in 1996. He was Japan's leading composer, an admirer of Debussy, Ravel, Messiaen and Berg, a friend of John Cage and Morton Feldman. He composed the music for over ninety films, including collaborations with Akira Kurosawa, Masaki Kobayashi, and Hiroshi Teshigahara. Toru was an expert on Western pop music and he also wrote books—from detective novels to serious commentaries on the arts and life—as well as music. He remains an inspiration for generations of composers worldwide.

Toru's music is like the wind—dancing with silence and often finding a magical stillness to balance his vast soundscape. From austere and abstract, through sublime transitions to a warmth that will make the sun rise in your heart, Toru's music sprang from his life experience with a sincerity that touched me deeply. His experience with and knowledge of the musics of the world was vast. He admired the sincerity of country music and had a great love for the art of the song. His spirit garden was the music of today:

> It seems to me that most contemporary music carefully avoids the past. I am not afraid of it. On the contrary, I need at the same time whatever is newest just as much as I need whatever is oldest. However, the unknown is found neither in the past, nor the future, but in reality, simply in the immediate present.
> —Toru Takemitsu

He said that his pieces were like Japanese gardens. His exquisite music welcomes the listener in—"a garden never spurns those who enter"—for contemplation, spiritual reflection, and pleasure for the senses. The titles of his pieces suggest images of nature and the elements—wind, rain, trees, water, sea, islands, birds.

> I feel a deep reverence for the precise workings and the great order in nature, and still wish to learn more from nature as I compose music.
> —Toru Takemitsu

Through sublime creativity and craftsmanship Toru brought the world closer together, establishing a unique voice and enriching the language of music. He had a preference for peaceful music, and in 1990 Nexus was blessed with a piece from the magical world of Toru's imagination. Commissioned to commemorate the 100th anniversary of Carnegie Hall, Toru wrote "From me flows what you call time" for Nexus and the Boston Symphony Orchestra and Seiji Ozawa. Seiji conducted the premiere in October 1990 in Carnegie Hall, that venerable palace of sound in New York City. Toru explained the title of the piece: "I suddenly imagined one hundred years of time flowing through this man-made space, so full of special meaning."

Toru Takemitsu lived what he called "The Miracle of Music," and described himself as "a gardener of sound."

> A garden is composed of various elements and sophisticated details that converge to form a harmonious whole. Each element does not exert its individuality, but achieves a state of anonymity...and that is the kind of music that I would like to create.
>
> —Toru Takemitsu

His music sings of nature and the life forces that touch us on a daily basis. Toru often said that if he could build a concert hall it would be called "The Miracle Box." For thirty years I have nurtured a dream of building a temple for sound, a concert hall whose bottom line is exquisite acoustics; a place where people can find a deep peace by simply listening. With Toru's passing I have felt a stronger impetus to realize the dream and dedicate it to the man, celebrating his inspired work. I would like to call this space "Mitsue." *Mitsue* is a word from the Cree language meaning meeting place. Music is a meeting place, a precious reconciliation of diverse elements and perceptions finding a unity in sound.

We are all richer for the work of Toru Takemitsu—always the positive spirit. The last letter I received from him, written from his hospital bed shortly before he died, contained the following message:

> Under no circumstances should we allow sorrow to close down our lives. Toru.

❖

Dear Toru:

Thank you for the lessons—for the friendship—for the joy—for a faith in me that set me free—your amazing generosity. I love the way you reached me when the need was really there, with lessons clear, sometimes severe, always delivered with care. As you continue to dance in my dreams—I am filled with love. The inspiration of your work is such a healing source for the family of humanity, and the sensitivity and generosity of your spirit is a constant source of benevolence.

MORE GUIDES

John Cage

Remembering a conversation: I asked John Cage what motivated him to compose. His response was characteristically simple: "Everything in creation has a spirit, and all you have to do to discover that spirit is to get it vibrating." Conversations with John were like taking your mind to the cleaners. He polished the old mirror, and for awhile the open mind would wonder—an experience for which I was consistently and eternally grateful.

Cage's writing for percussion peaked with his *Third Construction* in 1941—the year I was born. My first encounter with Cage was an experience I shared with my dad. We were watching a show on television called "I've Got a Secret." Garry Moore was the host, and a panel of four tried to guess the secret of the guests. As the curtain opened, we saw a table upon which were a radio, an electric fan, some pots and pans, and many common found objects. The guest was John Cage, and his secret was that he was going to make music with these objects. At the tender age of ten, I was convinced that I knew what music was, and I began to laugh and pooh-pooh this charlatan on the TV screen. Little did I know what precious seeds he was planting. Cage approached the table and began to explore the sounds, and I laughed even harder as my arrogance grew to ludicrous proportions.

Ten years later, as a student at Eastman, I was involved in a performance of a piece that John Cage had written for twelve radios. My experience with this piece changed my original perceptions about Cage, and I began to explore more of his music. I found myself completely charmed by his sonatas for prepared piano.

The assumption of understanding, attaching importance to an idea or to what one thinks, is a great disease of the mind.

The creative work of John Cage was often challenging and controversial, occasionally provoking spontaneous audience response and/or participation, depending on your point of view. Cage loved this spontaneity, getting the audience vibrating.

In the late 1970s and early 1980s Nexus performed an amalgamation of two works by John Cage. "Child of Tree" and "Branches" were conceptual works that shared a similar source in Cage's imagination. Both were concerned with the exploration of the sounds of vegetable matter, e.g., wood, leaves, twigs, plants, etc. After much experimentation and discussion with the composer, we decided to use cactus plants for the performances. Attaching contact microphones to the cactus plants allowed for the amplification of the sound that was produced when the spines of the plants were plucked. (Some cactus have strong spines of varying lengths, offering a variety of pitches and substantial resistance providing a strong rich sound and ease of performance, while others offer such a thick crop of wispy needle-like spines that performance is more challenging and at times even dangerous.) Due to the complications of transporting plants across international borders we always asked presenters to supply the cactus plants for concert performances.

In 1984 the Holland Festival supplied plants for the concert Nexus was giving at the Carre Theatre in Amsterdam. We were plucking away on the amplified plants when someone in the audience yelled, "Bullshit!" As we continued the piece I noticed a restlessness from Robin and watched as his color changed from various shades of red to purple until he exploded by shouting: "Cactus Shit!" The audience responded in a fit of laughter, a wonderful, spontaneous sonic event, removing all tension from the room and allowing us to finish the performance with a new concentration.

Laughter is a superb solvent for dissolving presumptions.

❖

The empty cup school of benevolent observation
   Everyday, every tune is a new journey
      There are no tools in the form of rules
         Trust your perceptions
         Trust your ears
           Trust the original idea
              Go with the Inspiration
                Empty cup is useful
                   Full cup is occupied
                      So it is with mind

Touch

    Touch is the process of getting things vibrating.
       Touch—the way we use energy to massage,
          to shape,
             to be tender,
                to love.
    A touch you can trust is a source of healing.

❖

    The physician must be experienced in many things,
    but most assuredly in rubbing.
                                 —HIPPOCRATES

❖

Healing through touch goes back thousands of years. Drummers access and explore sound through the synergy of touch and hearing. Touch is a transfer of energy. Hearing is the perception of the vibrations of the object touched, touching the ear drum. Experience brings a sensitivity to the myriad sonic possibilities that become part of the percussionist's collection of colors. Sounds range from very soft to very loud, from tiny to huge, from hot to cold, from dark to bright, from clear and precise to vague and mysterious, from lots of fundamental to lots of edge, from very hard to very gentle, from slow to fast, from short to long. Weave them into various permutations and the possibilities are infinite.

    Touch and sound are the fruit of our character. What we are is what we communicate.

Sound
The World of the Musician

Concert halls, like everything in nature, are each unique, and should remain so. When we institute rules and regulations that are designed to achieve good acoustics we are homogenizing everyone's unique vision and creative insight into a boring uniformity.

One of the joys of the road is performing in different acoustical spaces. New halls expand your experience with sound, generating new sensitivities. Old music sounds new again. Your instruments seem to find new qualities. The ensemble you are a part of takes on new characteristics, and the whole process of making music is somehow renewed.

Performing in a concert hall with great acoustics is paradise for a musician. Every sound that comes from your instrument is delivered **clearly** and **benevolently** and **without distortion** to every part of the space and back again to the performer in such a way that the musician falls in love with the sound, the source of that sound (the instrument), and, most important, the music.

"Clearly" means hearing all the different voices in the music, in balance, making for a tight ensemble. "Without distortion" means realistic feedback, hearing as is—reflecting the wide spectrum of harmonics—low to high, without favoring any particular range over another. "Benevolent" means that the energy needed to get your instrument to sing is not a challenge. Without a struggle, the physical tools of production are relaxed and the sound can blossom freely, enhancing and expanding the expressive range of your instrument.

A great acoustic equals ease of sound production equals a long career. A bad acoustic equals must work much harder equals a shorter career.

With great acoustics, every expression, from the softest, most intimate to the wailing of ecstasy, fills the hall without undue effort, generating a spontaneity and joy that is at the heart of loving.

❖

> There is a single magic
> a single power
> a single salvation
> and a single happiness
> and that is called Loving.
>
> — HERMANN HESSE

Nature

I was no stranger to Canada when I moved here in 1966 to join the Toronto Symphony Orchestra. Every summer from the time I was six my family had retreated to a cabin in south central Ontario on the Trent River, where we fished, explored the wilderness, and simply found a solitude. I was seduced completely by the tranquillity of living close to nature, so in the early 1970s I began looking for rural property and purchased some land in 1972, where I reside to this day with my wife, Jean.

Tranquillity
The healing power of stillness
Be still—and quiet
without intention

❖

I have devoted more than one day simply to the discovery of it.

— Paul Claudel

❖

Silence has the power to reform us
Sound can bring the mind to rest
Quiet observation
Repose knows

Develop attentiveness. As our single-mindedness develops, our concentration deepens and brings our focus to the present moment, leaving behind the past and the future. The more time we spend in the present the more relevant our work becomes and the more perceptive we become—perception itself yields insight.

Vision is simply the perception of opportunity.

Being there—as sound disappears—we are drawn to Now
Being less selective—and more attentive
Deepen the attention
Deepen the Spirit
Hear like a mirror

The Sound Environment—Urban versus Forest

Sound touches our lives on a daily basis in a very powerful way. With too much sound, too loud, perception becomes impaired. We are unable to relax. We must learn to create calm, quiet environments to balance the intensity of the contemporary urban soundscape.

To do anything well, it must be done with a quiet mind. We must create within the home a place of solitude. We must create within the workplace a calm, quiet environment where the imagination can flourish and productivity will not be interrupted by unwanted sounds. We must create within ourselves a being of calm attentiveness.

Technology has provided the tools that have led to the pollution of our urban and rural soundscapes. Sound delivery systems for music, advertising, and public service messages are doing the public little service, by providing an incessant stream of unwanted messages. The sound of machinery: cars, trucks, planes, chain saws, jet skis, snow-mobiles, tractors, weed-whackers, leaf blowers, etc. etc., multiplied hundreds of thousands of times in the city, equals stress. Raking leaves is a calming, beneficial exercise.

We can't go back to the stone age, but we can do many things to reduce the unhealthy levels of sound in our environment.

❖

Wilderness—the word itself is Music.

—EDWARD ABBEY

Benevolent Soundscape
— The vibrations we live with —

For most of my adult life I have been living in a garden of bells. Since my youth I have been attracted to the sounds of bells and gongs, from the great bronze temple bells of Asia to the church bells of Christendom. There's the incredible metallic joy of the whole Malay archipelago that bursts forth from Southeast Asia in the form of the gamelan orchestras of Indonesia.

Music helps us to concentrate or meditate, independent of thought. For centuries Buddhism has recognized the ability of sound to focus one's attention, and many extraordinary bells and various metallic sound sources of great sophistication have evolved from the numerous varieties and sects into which Buddhism has blossomed. Christianity has also had a substantial influence on the evolution of the bell, from altar bells and hand bell choirs to the carillons of the cathedrals.

Influenced by the insights and technology of R. Buckminster Fuller and the sublime thoughts of Native North Americans— which I'd read about in T.C. McLuhan's *Touch the Earth*, I decided that I wanted to live in a round, open space. So in 1972 I began a nest by building a four-phase geodesic dome, a hemisphere forty-feet in diameter. A third of the ground floor was for the kitchen, bathroom and a small study. Over these three areas spread a sleeping loft. The rest of the space was for music.

I hung hundreds of bells from the curved arc of the hemisphere. They were suspended from long strings, and when set in motion the natural pendulum action would continue for quite some time. The bells always created an unpredictable flow of sonorities beyond anticipation, and the natural ritard of the pendulum action flowed from activity to stillness through a gradual and serene diminuendo. Eventually the bells evolved into a nightly lullaby lasting from twenty to thirty minutes at bedtime as we drifted off into dreamland. It was wonderful to have an instrument that played itself into oblivion.

The long decay of a bell's sound takes one on a journey. As sound disappears into the now-ness that binds all ears together, we're transported by the ebb and flow from activity to stillness. As a musician I have always been fascinated by this disappearance of sound at the end of its natural decay. Welcome to Now!

Nature's soundscape is a tapestry of rhythms and sonorities that weave their magic as spontaneously and unpredictably as the first flower of spring. Throughout the world, legends pay tribute to the sounds of nature as our source of music. In China the *erhu* has a repertoire that has come directly from the songs of birds. The Japanese *shakuhachi* finds its source in the wind. An Indonesian tradition tells of children discovering strange objects on the beach; elders were summoned and the unusual objects were moved to the village. The elders studied with the birds to learn how to make music with these new objects.

At home I am privileged to observe and often participate in the amazing variations that flow from the immediate environment. Every spring four varieties of frogs join the orchestre de la pond, bringing to the band a passion, intensity, and decibel level that can only come from a force as old as the universe, the urge to mate. In the spring, when the birds are establishing their territory, I've played duets with woodpeckers on the cedar posts around the garden. The woodlands of my home have stretched me from the intimacy of the music of insects to the vastness of infinity for a ceiling.

❖

> The Peepers in the spring
>   can show us how to sing
> The Wind is strong and filled with song
> Birds bless our day with their winsome way
> And not a sound comes through as wrong

❖

> Act in the knowledge of our oneness
> Snowflake kisses stone—we are never alone
> Warm rock charming a song from the whippoorwill

❖

Listen to the Wind

"The man who sat on the ground in his tipi
meditating on life and its meaning,
accepting the kinship of all creatures
and acknowledging unity
with the universe of things,
was infusing into his being
the true essence of civilization.
And when native man left off this form of
development his humanization was retarded."

—Chief Luther Standing Bear

❖

Build your nest where you are inspired to be humble.
Create a sanctuary that offers the timelessness of
    childhood, and the unity of joyful play.
Lose yourself by loving what you do.

❖

In 1972 I spent two wonderful weeks living in the bell tower of St. Mark's Church in Niagara-on-the-Lake, Ontario. Participation in a series of concerts brought me to the oldest Anglican parish in Canada, established in 1792. The bell tower, made of stone and timbers, was at the north end of the building, towering above the entrance to the sanctuary. Through a small door behind the organ loft was a small empty room. It had a plain wooden floor and ceiling with a hole for a large rope leading up to the main bell of the tower. The stone walls were unadorned except for a ladder that led to the carillon above. The space was about 8' x 8'—enough for a sleeping bag and a pile of clothes. Permission to crash there was granted by the Venerable Reverend Hugh Maclean, a very wise and sensitive man. Aside from rehearsals and concerts I found myself alone in this place of worship. Climbing up among the bells became a regular exercise, especially at dawn, to watch the sun rise and to listen to the wind—coaxing harmonics from the massive bells. By the age of thirty I had come to appreciate the experience of being still and alone and sitting quietly in empty concert halls and other places of worship; so having access to this beautiful sanctuary, twenty-four-hours a day for two weeks, was a wonderful opportunity to meditate, pray, and play with the wonder and joy of awakening.

    From Roshi Philip Kapleau at the Rochester (New York) Zen Center I had learned the importance of resting the mind, and had begun the practice of zazen. A growing interest in Zen Buddhism was beginning to challenge my life in music as I wandered in search of myself. When I arrived at St. Mark's I found myself at the proverbial (self-inflicted) fork in the road. My life in, and love for, music represented one path, and the monastic life of a Buddhist monk represented the other. The seriousness of my dialogue with myself had created this canyon in my consciousness.

Choice—the discriminating beast—had raised its head. The solitude of the church provided a rich environment to ponder the question, and one quiet afternoon I found myself knocking at the door to the manse in search of guidance. Rev. Maclean welcomed me with a smile and said, "I've been expecting you." The anticipation excited me and I poured out my heart to him, trying to share my state of mind. He rose from his chair and walked into the library where he reached for a book and returned to his desk. Opening a volume on church music, he underlined a sentence and passed the book to me, and I read,

"No one is more humble than the artist before his art."

Tears of joy began to flow at the extraordinary release taking place. We both wept with joy as I danced around the pastor's study. This was not a matter of choice, but a realization that music was and always had been a natural meditation—often providing a deep samadhi, a realization that the creative spirit is an ancient pathway to a more universal consciousness. Peace of mind comes from simple acceptance, including accepting ourselves.

❖

> Your treasure house is within.
> It contains all you will ever need.
> Use it fully instead of seeking vainly outside yourself.
>
> —Hui Hai

Music Education and Performance

Today there seems to be too much emphasis placed on technique and winning competitions. As art imitates life, maybe this is a simple reflection of our technologically driven culture.

Setting students or young musicians off on the path of discovery is the heart of learning to learn.

Allowing young talent to be whatever it can be instead of what we think it should be.

To young artists I say—Touch Me.

Technique is a means not an end.

Music is not about proving yourself, it's about finding yourself and sharing your discovery.

❖

It is the duty of musicians to bring the music to the audience, not the fact that they can play their instruments.

— Adolf Busch

❖

There are many schools in the university of life, and among the finest is travel. I think it would be beneficial to offer those students who have demonstrated a certain level of responsibility, and have reached the age where they think they know it all, the opportunity to experience the world and see how other cultures spend their daily lives. Of course, this age (fourteen to seventeen) would vary with each individual. For some, the life of a wandering vagabond would be perfect.

Others would prefer a month here, a month there, with time at home to digest and absorb the lessons. Economy travel-passes and accommodation would be provided for from one to two years. Living within a budget would be required. An expansion of the exchange student program could function well within this program. After this experience the students would be encouraged to pursue their dreams and realize their potential at appropriate centers of expertise, whether enrolling in institutions or apprenticing to a master in their chosen field of endeavor. Pursuing what they want to achieve, not what some educational, social, political or religious tradition thinks they should be doing.

Exchange between cultures is such a powerful tool for peace. When we come to understand each other we find a common heart beating for humanity. Dancing to the rhythms of life and singing praises to God, celebrating the cycles of creation. We all long to be what we are. Through unification with the vitality of life. In sharing this preciousness we find love and understanding and wisdom.

Consider the lessons of the tree:
    the seed knows what to become
        natural intelligence—staggering ramifications
            rooted in the organic wholeness of the
            universe.

            Nurture the Seed
        Don't teach—share discovery

Life is so much more than we know
    the plants will teach you all you need to grow
        the mighty tree says—let it be
            patience—be still as my branches reach aloft
                quiet says the moss—I'll show you soft.

❖

I am what nature has predisposed me to be.

—LEONARDO DA VINCI

❖

What is it in the human condition that allows us to sacrifice unique individual expressions to the trendy homogenization of styles we call fashion?

History has some lessons. For example, by the sixth century A.D., each congregation of monks had developed its own chant. Expressing their collective spirits, the monks responded to each other and to the acoustical environment of the chapel or sanctuary where the chanting took place. Unique intonation, scales, and/or modes evolved quite naturally. Each monastery, each collection of aspirants, had achieved their own **sincere** form of worship.

Well, along came Gregory I who selected his favorite chants and created a unified setting of the liturgy for all Catholic churches, and Gregorian Chant was born. Was this a sincere and righteous effort to unify the Church? Was this the power of the papal position saying let's do what I like? Whatever the motivation, it was not in harmony with the natural order of things.

Is it loneliness that allows us to assume that what we think is good for everyone? Is it a need to belong, a yearning for unification for ourselves? A view of the past shows us that tradition is often challenged by the reality of nowness. We can rationalize this challenge in many ways. If we embrace change the challenge of tradition is viewed positively; if we cling to tradition the challenge can be viewed as negative.

Around the world young musical talent is leaving the traditional village and is migrating to large cities to embrace the music of a much larger environment—the planet. The negative view of this migration sees the challenge to the local musical traditions, an imminent warning of the local music becoming endangered.

The migration and integration of traditional musics into the music of another culture is often met with cries of cultural appropriation. The creative spirit of performers and composers is immune to these negative views. Their vision allows them to embrace the process as the natural growth of a new music. The evolution of a universal language (popular music) has positive ramifications as the people of the world reach out to communicate and attempt to understand each other. The most balanced view would probably be to accept the lessons of history and see that this process of migrating insight has always been a part of the human condition, in all processes of life.

❖

Openness
Seeing through every question without trying to discredit anyone or anything...

—Thomas Merton

Reverence—The stately determination to make something worthy of the materials and the Moment.

—Deng Ming-Dao

Knowledge, which comes from real life experience, is something that we can use.

Belief is something that uses us.

We are standing on a whale fishing for minnows.

— POLYNESIAN

Perception is an act of surrender.

— GRETEL EHRLICH

Seeing with the Ears

When I drop something I usually locate what I've dropped by the sound of its impact—Listening like a wolf. The wolf observes the meadow in search of a meal. The ears perceive the various voices of the area, not only the beginning of the sound and its duration and interaction with other voices, but the end of the sound as well. Remember the experience of walking through the grass in the evening. The crickets are singing, and as we walk near them their voices disappear. The naturalist writer R.D. Lawrence calls these areas "islands of silence." The wolf knows that these islands of silence can be created by a meal wandering through the tall grasses.

In the late seventies and early eighties the great jazz artist Red Norvo often came to Toronto to play at Bourbon Street, a club on Queen St. West. I got to know Red by hanging out with him during the breaks and trying to get him to talk about his influential career in jazz. I was always fascinated by the fact that Red never looked at the vibraphone when he was performing. He would just stare straight ahead into the audience. When I asked him about this he looked me right in the eye and said, "Music always sounds much better than it looks."

R. Murray Schafer, prolific composer, author, educator, environmentalist, scholar, and visual artist, is one of Canada's most powerful and prodigious creative sources. Murray has composed in many genres, and many of his works reflect his interest in Eastern philosophy, mysticism, and ritual.

In May of 1983, thirty-three actors, singers, dancers, and musicians worked together in the first production of RA,

Murray's eleven-hour sunset-to-sunrise music-theater epic, based on the story of the Egyptian sun god Ra. The audience, or more correctly, the initiates, are led through a series of events that transformed the mythology into a real, intimate experience.

It was my good fortune to be part of this production, performing a duet with Maureen Forrester, the legendary contralto whose voice and musical line have a direct and powerful link to the heart. The duet was titled "Aria of Amente-Nufe," after the goddess who symbolizes the West and the uplifting of the soul (appropriate casting of the lady whose vocal artistry has touched humanity in such a positive way). It was my pleasure to accompany the goddess with seventy-five bells, gongs and cymbals. Murray created a haunting duet that was designed to awaken the initiates from their meditation, or rest, that took place from 2:40 to 3:30 am. For ten performances of this magical music Maureen and I had to crawl very quietly out on to a catwalk where the bells and gongs were set up, without disturbing the meditators. One morning as we were crawling out to the performance area at 3:25 a.m., one of the initiates let out an incredibly resonant and sincere snore; it tickled Maureen's fancy and I could see her begin vibrating as she tried to suppress her giggles. All performers learn to suppress laughter, sneezes, coughs and any other involuntary outbursts that occur during performances and recording sessions, usually at great physical discomfort. Given Maureen's powerful presence I was unable to resist the force of her giggling and we were both swept away into a fit of suppressed laughter that gave a new and unexpected energy to the opening of the wakeup-call duet.

There is a bond musicians share, and once touched and inspired by each other a love is generated that transcends all the challenges life offers up.

Music—the family art

From 1987 to 1994 I was alternating between Nexus, World Drum Festivals and playing timpani with the Boston Symphony. The symphony orchestra, Nexus, and all the other variations of ensemble music that have been part of my life in the last forty years are a musical family that has inspired me as a performer, as a composer, and as a member of the family of humanity, to appreciate the preciousness of family in generating a positive spirit.

One of my most memorable and moving experiences of the art of ensemble took place in Madrid, Spain, in late November of 1961. The Eastman Philharmonia, an orchestra of eighty-seven students from the Eastman School of Music, was on a three-month tour of Europe, the Middle East, and the USSR. In Madrid, we were performing Stravinsky's suite from "The Firebird." In the middle of the "Infernal Dance of King Kastchei," all the lights went out. The place was pitch black. The orchestra continued to play from memory and we finished the Infernal Dance in the dark. The audience gasped, and then with silence engulfing us all, the bassoon began the haunting "Berceuse." All of this, coming out of the darkness, this wonderful trust in the music, and trust in the sense of ensemble that comes when a group of people share a reverence, a devotion, a love; this is the real fabric of family. To this day when I hear the horn singing the solo line from the "Berceuse" my soul is on its knees, and I'm grateful that I've been able to make my way in life doing what I love to do.

Music teaches us that the preciousness of family lies in the fact that we are centered and strengthened by our relatedness. The attraction and the balance of opposites in the ebb and flow of relationships challenge us and lead to growth. We must balance the individual's freedom to flower with the responsibility of the parts to the whole. Reasonableness comes from knowing that we are all in this together. Individuality equals unique perceptions and unique understanding, and so we inspire and challenge each other. Moderation, working in harmony with our life lessons, is essential in navigating the ancient pathways of responsibility and reasonableness.

Composers, performers, conductors, and audiences all have unique perceptions and individual ideas about every aspect of music. Melody, Line, Color, Harmony, Pulse, all conjure up images from our unique perspectives. Music reconciles differences and offers us the possibility of unification.

TRAVEL

Travel seems to unravel the prejudices, assumptions, and misconceptions one assimilates in one's native environment. Armed with my naive idealistic optimism and my American education, I had just completed a three-month crash course in the amazing diversity and beauty of the human condition during the Eastman Philharmonia tour. I experienced first hand the love and genuine warmth of all the cultures I encountered. Making friends in every country, I felt the generosity of those who were poor in material assets but so rich in spirit. The wonderful sensitivity to and appreciation of the arts that is so much a part of every culture was a real inspiration. Three months of Real Life Experience made me a citizen of the world.

Leningrad

February 21, 1962—The Eastman Philharmonia was in Leningrad (St. Petersburg) and had just finished its final concert of the three-month tour. We were scheduled to take the overnight train from Leningrad to Moscow. There was an urgency, after packing our instruments, to return to the hotel across the street from the concert hall, gather our things and board the buses to the train station. The street in front of the hall was jammed with people. Audience and musicians exchanged greetings, trying to make their way through the crowd. I must admit I was trying to negotiate my way through the crush of people like a horse wearing blinders. I was focused on the lobby of the hotel where I could buy a bottle of champagne to share with my sweetheart so we could celebrate our love and pursue our passion on the train to Moscow. Stepping off the sidewalk to cross the street I was approached by a middle-aged couple. The man thrust a folded paper into my hand. I was so absorbed in my erotic self-indulgent fantasies that I continued across the street, clutching the folded paper in my hand, and I had almost reached the other side of the street when it hit me like a burning match reaching my fingers: This couple had given me this note, and I hadn't even acknowledged them or read the message. Stopping in my tracks, I read:

> "Thank you very much for your wonderful concerts! We congratulate you with your Friendship. Our best wishes to you and your people."
>
> The Labellos Family—21.02.62

I turned and scanned the evening concert crowd making its way home to try and find the couple that had given me the note. Finally I saw them way down the block. They had watched me read the message and when our eyes met they waved with enthusiasm. My heart leapt up and I waved with joy. That the communication had been confirmed was wonderful, but did not assuage the regret that welled up inside me for missing out on the moment, as I saw my self-indulgent ways for what they were.

Invariably we see that our idea of what should be keeps us from what is.

Leningrad had carved its way into my life with an intensity that would never leave. The Hermitage, the Labellos family, my new friend Nicolai Moskolenko (the young timpanist of the Leningrad Philharmonic), the statue of Pushkin in the park near the hotel, all conspired to haunt my memories.

More Travel

A life in music is a life of travel. In 1970 Robin Engelman and I set out on a journey that would take us to Japan, the Philippines, Java, Bali, and Hong Kong. The purpose of our visit to Japan was performances in the Space Theater at Expo 70 in Osaka. The theater was part of the Expo pavilion of the Iron and Steel Corporation of Japan. Performers, composers and critics from around the world gathered in Osaka for concerts, serious discussions, and the casual dialogue that is part of the social life of musicians. The Space Theater was designed and guided artistically by Toru Takemitsu. The performance parameters were new and inspired: a round theater with fifteen-hundred speakers in the floor, walls, and ceiling; all controlled by computer so the sound could be programmed to move about the theater. The sound could begin in the center of the floor, expand to the walls, travel up the walls and out the ceiling. Sound could flow around the walls of the theater, and much much more. A state-of-the-art laser light system was part of the design, and laser phases as well as laser beams were used with startling effect. A laser phase creates a wall of light that can be tinted and projected to the stage to create a myriad of effects, including the division of the performance space into a variety of architectural spaces, using walls of light.

Lucas Foss made interesting use of the laser light installation with a piece he called "Map." Each musician was given a proscribed path through a series of spatial areas created by the laser phases. Wandering through walls of light into new dimensions the musicians would encounter each other, pause, and create a new musical moment. Then they would continue on their paths, meeting up with other members of the ensemble, and other combinations of instruments would be heard, as the performers reacted to the new environment of light and sound.

Inspired performances and interesting dialogue between composers and critics, and between performers and critics, led me to understand that in Japan the role of the critic is more that of an informed commentator, as opposed to being a source of judgment, which is the prevalent tradition in Western cultures. In Japan, the critic, or commentator, is accepted as an equal part of the cultural family.

The trip Robin and I made to the Philippines was one of exploration. From Jose Maceda, the wonderful Philippine composer and friend of Takemitsu, we received a contact at the University in Manila, someone who could help us in our quest for traditional music and instruments of the Philippine people. It was suggested that we travel to the island of Mindanao and make our way to Marawi City, where we would be assisted by

Abdullah T. Madale. Abdullah was a prince in the Muslim culture that predominates on the island of Mindanao, and a leader in his community. He was also the Acting Dean of External Studies at the university outside of Marawi City.

After speaking with Professor Madale on the phone from Manila, Robin and I made our travel arrangements and were off to the jungles of Mindanao. It was a short hop from Manila to Cebu where we picked up a smaller plane that took us to Mindanao, a mountainous, densely forested island just north of the equator. The plane skimmed over a plantation of pineapple trees and landed on a narrow airstrip that was surrounded by dense growth.

Robin and I were the only passengers to leave the plane. The airstrip was deserted except for a black limousine and two men in black suits standing on either side of the limo. Each man held a machine gun. The plane took off immediately, and Robin and I looked at each other, wondering what we had gotten ourselves into. We walked past the limo and the two armed men in total silence; all we heard was the sound of the plane (our only means of escape) disappearing into the distance. We found ourselves in a small area that had been cleared for parking next to the airstrip, pondering our next move, when a jeep appeared and pulled up alongside us, the driver inquiring about our identity. He had been instructed to pick us up and return directly to Dr. Madale at the university.

After a long drive through the jungle, Marawi City appeared in an opening in the dense vegetation. It looked like a nineteenth-century pioneer logging settlement. Muddy streets and wooden sidewalks on the main street provided access to the shops, all made from the same rough-cut unpainted local lumber. The driver of the jeep had seemed nervous from the time he picked us up at the airstrip, and he zipped through

Marawi City very quickly as his anxiety quickened. Soon we arrived at the university campus and the jeep pulled up in front of the guest house. The driver took us inside and sent someone to fetch Dr. Madale. When Madale arrived he explained that there had been a lot of unrest lately. Militant guerrilla organizations were working to establish an independent Muslim state on the island of Mindanao, and the day before our arrival a student had been killed on the university campus. Dr. Madale's attempts to reach us in Manila to discourage our visit had failed, and with our arrival he was quite concerned for our well-being. He told us not to leave the guest house under any circumstances and promised to return.

In the evening two jeeps pulled up in front of the guest house and people began unloading instruments and fabrics, turning the large front room of the guest house into a mini-bazaar. Because of the possible dangers in wandering around Marawi City, Dr. Madale had arranged for some musicians and dancers to come to the guest house to perform for us. The instruments were all percussion: several deep gongs with a unique design encouraged a strong low fundamental pitch of short duration; small tuned gongs called *kulintang*, played by women as was the tradition, were assigned the melodic role; and a goblet drum about three feet tall assumed the traditional role of timekeeper, while the low gongs danced in hocket patterns, supporting the rhythmic structure of the music and adding the low pitches as a bass line supporting the melody in the kulintang.

The performance in the guest house whet our appetites. Turned on by the new sounds, we pleaded with our host to allow us to explore outside the university campus. Dr. Madale said he would try to arrange a trip to Marawi City, but not until much later in the evening. Eventually he returned with the jeep and we were off to the old part of the town where a friend had agreed to allow Robin and me to examine the musical instruments he had for sale. We entered an old shop filled with antiques and artifacts. It was late, after normal shop hours, and the lighting was almost nonexistent. One dim light on a counter at the rear of the shop brought a glow to the faces of two women, their mouths red from chewing betel nut, making music with two bamboo mouth-harps. The sounds were enchanting, and the simplicity of the music was refreshing.

We bought a few gongs, a set of kulintang, and the bamboo mouth-harps that were being played so beautifully. Fearing for our security if we went anywhere else in the city, our host returned us to the guest house. Abdulla's concerns for our well-being were genuine and he suggested that we try to leave Mindanao as soon as possible. Four large gongs and two sets of kulintang had now become part of our baggage, and the only available transport from the island was by plane or boat. Having explored the possibilities, Robin and I decided to travel by boat so that we could stop at some of the other smaller islands and make our way to Cebu where we could catch a plane to Manila.

Early the next morning, with the instruments all packed in their traditional rattan and reed basket cases, we were off in the jeep. Speeding along the roads through the jungle, the driver seemed even more concerned than the day before. Was there a real and present danger? I was beginning to feel like a basket-case myself. Smelling the ocean, the senses came to attention, and soon the road ended at a wooden pier that extended out into Iligan Bay. Nothing else, no boat, no people, no building. Our driver disappeared into the jungle—God knows where he went—and returned to inform us that there was no boat this week. Looking at his watch he said that there was a plane leaving the airstrip in thirty minutes. "How far is the airstrip?" Robin asked. "About forty-five minutes," was the reply, as the driver put the jeep into warp speed and began racing through the dense vegetation.

Pushing the envelope of speed has never been my idea of a good time. Doing it in an open jeep with no seat belts on a rough road was balanced only by the assumed need to get the hell out of there, yet the excitement of this race with fate had a certain calm about it. Arriving at the airstrip, the driver drove right to the plane and told us to board immediately, promising to get the instruments on the plane. Fortunately we had open return tickets to Manila, and as the flight attendant approached us I was hoping the plane was indeed headed north, as opposed to being the monthly flight to Zamboanga or Tawitawi.

Good fortune was smiling on us and in three hours Robin and I were standing at the registration counter at the Manila Hilton Hotel—two hippies complete with sandals and beards, backpacks and rattan baskets filled with gongs. We looked like an ad for American Express, and indeed when I presented my credit card to the gentleman behind the counter his expression became much more accommodating.

Our previous stay in Manila earlier in the week had been a big disappointment. The Timberland Hotel where we'd stayed was run-down and dirty, and the rooms had not been cleaned, nor the toilets flushed. Our first trip in the elevator at the Timberland was one for the highlight reel. A young man entered the elevator and began combing his hair in the mirror; a thirty-eight caliber revolver was holstered in his back pocket, and when he had finished with his hair he turned and asked us if we would like to buy his sister.

As we flew from Mindanao to Manila it was easy to agree that we would treat ourselves to a better hotel. Our first action upon entering our room at the Hilton was to challenge room service to satisfy our appetites.

A call to the Canadian Embassy secured the name and phone number of a reliable shipping company that could transport the gongs and kulintang home to Toronto. After making the proper shipping arrangements we were off to Singapore. One of the great cultural crossroads in the world, Singapore and its markets, we thought, would contain many interesting instruments from Asia and the Pacific region. We had been warned many times that we would not be allowed to enter Singapore because of our beards and long hair, but hope springs eternal and we thought we would give it a shot. However, within five minutes of leaving the plane in Singapore we found ourselves in the transit lounge waiting for a flight to Jakarta.

> Needing is greeding—wanting is hunting for self-satisfaction—reaction to fiction friction.
>
> (Jakarta–1970)

"A cultural nightmare" was my immediate reaction to Jakarta. The clash between contemporary urban culture, with all its technology and cutting edge capitalism, and the ancient and sublime tradition of living in harmony with Nature and the will of all the gods, had created a quagmire of conflict and confusion. The chasm between rich and poor seemed insurmountable, and the inability of the bottom-line market forces to find any degree of harmony with the natural world and the world of the human spirit was obvious and distressing. Our hotel room in 1970 Jakarta cost fifty dollars a night. The average salary of an Indonesian worker in a shoe factory making products for export was fifty dollars a *year*. Yes, a year. One pair of those shoes might sell for fifty dollars in North America. How does one reconcile this form of exploitation?

Travel has allowed me to experience first hand the inequities of corporate exploitation of cheap labor in developing countries. There must be a better, more humane way to sustain production, to assist developing nations, and to maintain established production centers at home without disturbing existing labor forces for the sake of more profits from inexpensive labor elsewhere. All of this would take cooperation, as opposed to competition; not very available in the bottom-line market place.

Couldn't we invest in and encourage the ingenuity and creativity of local cultures so that unique products of distinction are created? Do all the developing countries of the world have to contribute to the homogenization of footwear by making sneakers? Do the garment districts of the world have to migrate to the poorest labor force to feed the fashion industry?

We know our system is not working for all of our people. We know we should fix things. Yet we argue forever as to how and what should be done—when and where. We do so little for humanity and so much for the market place.

This all reminds me of the internal dialogue of the individual. We know what we have to do for our own good and the good of others. We know when we're wrong, yet we rationalize and discourse within ourselves, constantly keeping the mind active and occupied to the point where we miss the point. We don't perceive the opportunity to change our ways, and wonder why we can't find time to do the things we really want to do. Perception comes from attentiveness, which comes from a quiet mind.

One of the attractions of mind-altering substances like alcohol, cannabis, or any other so-called recreational drugs, is the temporary vacation from concern that they provide. For many people, the slowing down of the activity of the mind can be interpreted as a form of euphoria. For others, this change in the activity of the mind can be discomforting and dangerous. The point that is important here is: slowing down! Slowing down the activity of the mind and developing attentiveness can be achieved through meditation. Slowing down the competitive rush for wealth and power. Slowing down the traffic. Slowing down the pace of your daily life. Take time to smell the shit in the air and understand how it got there.

Humanity cries out for love and understanding, forgiveness of debt, and a real need to harness our greed. With moderation comes the ability to share.

But enough of this ranting. Soon Robin and I were flying on Garuda Airlines on our way to Jogjakarta, the ancient cultural capital of Java. Leaving behind the urban madness of Jakarta, we entered into the sublime world of the *gamelan* (the musical ensembles of Java and Bali). Metallic percussion instruments predominate in the gamelans of Indonesia. Tuned gongs, metallaphones, xylophones, cymbals, bells, and drums, are joined by *suling* (bamboo flutes) and the *rebab*, an ancient and expressive string instrument. I have been touched deeply by the expressive range of the musicians of Indonesia, their spontaneity, and the extraordinary joy in their performance.

One morning as we were wandering outside of Jogja we came upon a group of children making music. It was like a kindergarten gamelan. Upon inquiring I discovered that their method of passing on the tradition was to have every young musician learn every part to every piece of music. Not just to know all the parts, but to be able to play all the parts. This accounts for the amazing spontaneous flexibility of their musical expression. The music is the conductor, and everyone knows all the parts. Can you imagine a symphony orchestra with that kind of understanding?

>Slowly Quietly Gently—Smile from Source
>Quiet Market—softly busy
>Beyond batik bargain—Woman Being
>Smile melts all to one
>>Life Smells Ringing
>>Wells of Singing Smiles
>>Bringing miles of peaceful people
>All Grace
>>comes from one place
>>–one face–one space—NOW

>>>>>(Jogjakarta–1970)

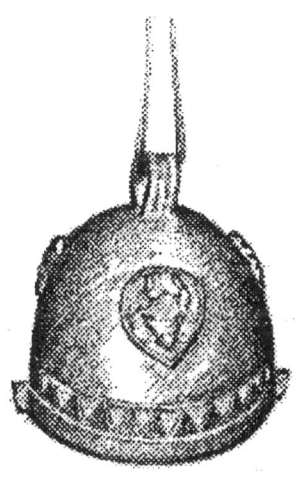

Transfixed by the smile of a beautiful woman selling batik fabric in one of the markets in Jogja, I was drawn from my transfixion by an exclamation from Robin. He had discovered a man selling brass oxen bells. Four different sizes of bells were stacked into neat golden pyramids reflecting the intense afternoon sun. Before long we had the bells spread out on the ground, attempting to find the sounds and pitches that would create scales or modes. Each size had a limited range and four of each seemed to create an interesting sixteen-tone instrument. All those brass bells in a shoulder bag also created some not-so-interesting shoulder pain. A quiet lane off the market place led us to a shop that had gamelan instruments. Several gongs and four sets of sarong bars were added to our heavy metal collection. A nearby shop supplied a large suitcase and cardboard boxes, and we retired to the hotel for some serious packing.

The following day was a pilgrimage to Borobudur. Described by some as the most significant monument in the southern hemisphere, the grandeur of Borobudur is beyond description, equal to that of Sanchi and Ajanta in India, or Angkor-Vat and Bayon in Cambodia. The site of Borobudur is ideal: Situated in the heart of Java, it is surrounded by mountains to the south and southwest, and by four volcanoes to the north, northeast, and northwest. Rice fields in all shades from green to gold, whispering bamboo trees, and the songs of many-colored birds create a serene and peaceful environment. Borobudur is one of the greatest Buddhist sanctuaries in the world. It was constructed on a hill about A.D. 800 during the reign of the Cailendra dynasty by the devotees of Mahayana Buddhism.

The monument's design combines the forms of the stupa, the temple mountain, and the mandala. Borobudur encloses a hill and consists of five square terraces graduating in size, crowned by three successively smaller circular terraces, the whole topped by the main stupa centered in the last terrace. The upper circular terraces are open and carry seventy-two bell-shaped stupas containing meditative Buddhas half visible through the perforated stonework. Ascending and circumnavigating the terraces, with all the stone-relief work, is a journey through Buddhist cosmology, the life of the Buddha, and the ascending stages of enlightenment.

Completing the climb to the upper terrace, we paused to rest. The view was awesome in any direction, inside or out. The years, the effort, the devotion involved in creating such a sanctuary inspires the imagination.

When a person sets to work, the human soul calms down.
— THOMAS CARLYLE

Suddenly we began to hear unusual sounds floating in the gentle breezes—haunting, other-worldly music. Eventually realizing that the sounds were floating up from the area of the main entrance, we began our descent to discover their source. Vendors were playing their bamboo flutes and demonstrating their bamboo tops. The tops were all different sizes, having vent holes that produced a singing tone when the top was spinning. From the distance of the upper terrace, the drone of the tops and the flutes sounded like the music of the spheres. The dialogue of the souvenir vendors hawking their wares had brought us down to earth.

The next morning Robin and I were to fly from Jogjakarta to Bali. The taxi took us to the airport terminal, which turned out to be a large house, probably built by the Dutch at some time during their long occupation of Indonesia. Walking in the front door we passed a man who checked our tickets and pointed to the back door across the room. Walking through the back door we sat on the steps to wait for the plane to arrive. It was a quiet morning. While we waited, Bach's "Air on a G String" began to permeate the airstrip from a cranked-up speaker. Suddenly, I was transported on a non-stop trip, operated by Universal Connections, to my memory of rehearsing, performing, and recording this music with Pablo Casals conducting the Marlboro Music Festival Orchestra in 1964, which had been an early confirmation of my life on the altar of Music. What an amazing influence sound has upon consciousness.

In the late-fifteenth century, Islam was spreading across the Indian subcontinent, through Sumatra and into Java. Many Javanese artists were unhappy with Islam's restrictions on artistic expression and migrated east to the island of Bali. For five centuries Bali has remained in cultural isolation, immune to the influences of either Islam or Christianity, firmly set in the religion and rich cultural tradition of Hinduism. For five hundred years Bali has flourished, like an art colony, where music, dance, drama, painting, and wood carving have all blossomed and played a vital role in everyday life. Most villages have their own recreational music clubs as well as gamelans that participate in the ancient rituals and spiritual traditions of the community. No two gamelans are tuned alike, and the differences can be substantial. Each ensemble creates its own tonal world, often finding fascinating, exotic (to our Western well-tempered ears) intervals and methods of tuning.

In 1959 I had heard a recording of music from Bali. The dream of the pilgrimage began to grow within me then, and I knew that someday, some way I would find my way to the magic Island that Nehru called "the morning of the world." Robin and I rented a traditional Balinese shelter on the beach at Sanur for nine dollars a night. The shelter had three walls with openings for light and breeze. The fourth side of the structure was completely open and faced the ocean. Walking along the beach we came upon a large covered pavilion where a performance of the Ketchak (Monkey Chant) was about to begin. The performance space was part of a resort complex so we sat down, ordered a libation, and waited for the event to unfold. Unfold indeed! Never in my life have I been so utterly absorbed and so totally captured by a performance experience. The synergy of the drama, the dance, and the chanting-chattering voices was riveting. The rhythmic interplay of the voices was trance-like, and several times during the presentation performers had to be helped out of their trance state by elders who kept a close watch on them. The drama was over, the audience was gone except for Robin and me. We looked at each other—silently—sharing. Standing to leave, we realized that neither of us had touched our drinks. Performance had been redefined—Life transformed.

Robin met Injoman Suardana, a young man who was working at one of the resorts in the Sanur beach area, and told him of our interest in the instruments of the gamelan. The next day we were on our way to his home in the village of Tihingan-Klungkung, in the mountains where the people of his village made the gongs, reong, gender, and cymbals that we were seeking. Our journey took us away from the tourists of Sanur beach and the bustle of Denpasar. In the village of Ubud every home was like an art gallery showing the work of local painters. The village of Mas was home for many fine wood carvers and was reputed to have the finest Ketchak dance on the island. The narrow road meandered around the hills and up into the mountains through a miracle of landscape artistry that sparkled with centuries of living in harmony with Nature. Arriving at Tihingan we were greeted by Suardana's family. One of the elders demonstrated the *gender* that was designed for the music of the Wayang Shadow Puppet Drama, so popular in the Balinese culture. A pair of these instruments (metallaphones with a range of two pentatonic octaves) is the main musical support for the puppet drama. The gender player's touch was so elusive that my perception seemed impaired. Not until years later, after actually performing with musicians from Bali and Java, did I realize that it was simply a matter of dynamics. The soft end of the sound spectrum is very sophisticated in their acoustic performance, as is the loud end, particularly in Bali, making for a very broad expressive range.

After hearing the variety of instruments from the village we were given a tour of the production facilities. It was a fascinating experience to observe the making of the large gongs. Averaging somewhere between three and four feet in diameter, these large bronze instruments are the foundation of the gamelan sound. Two young boys were singing and dancing as they worked the bellows to raise the temperature of the fire. Large tongs lifted the glowing metal from the fire and placed it on a large, round, flat stone table. Five men with sledge hammers began to strike the glowing metal, each in turn gradually getting faster as the man with the tongs turned the metal and controlled the evolution of its shape and temperament. When all the heat was beaten out of the metal it was returned to the fire. The boys continued their song and dance, and the fire began to respond to the bellows. When the metal was again glowing it was returned to the stone and the hammers repeated their amazing accellerando as they tempered the metal. This cycle was repeated many, many times in the creation of the gong.

Having completed the production tour we ordered some instruments and agreed on a price and time of delivery to Canada. Thanking our hosts and preparing for departure, we were approached by some of the women of the village in their beautiful sarongs, who presented us with arm loads of fresh fruits.

The music of Indonesia enchanted, inspired, and impressed me as a most sublime and sophisticated evolution of the art of touching—to express in sound what is in the heart.

Robin and I then returned to Japan, and were in Osaka along with the Lyric Arts Trio—Robert Aitken, Marion Ross, and Mary Morrison—representing the Toronto new music scene. Robin had bought a sarong in Indonesia, and I remember how excited he was about wearing it to perform in—a new horizon in mobility because the long tight skirt severely restricted his ability to walk.

Return to Leningrad

I returned to Leningrad in 1973, touring with the San Francisco Symphony, and the great city of Peter the Great did not disappoint. My good friend Nicolai embraced me with hugs and kisses. We had not seen each other since 1963 when the Leningrad Philharmonic had toured North America, and Nicolai had not expected to find me in his hometown. His enthusiasm swept me off my feet. Robin was on the tour as well, and Nicolai transported us to his favorite restaurant, "Baku," where he proceeded to fill us up with Armenian brandy and Georgian wine and the wonderful food of Azerbaijan. One of the most difficult social negotiations in life is to try to decline a drink from a Russian friend, so although I had not had any alcohol in my system for many years I went with the flow of our celebration of friendship. By mid-afternoon Robin and I were completely hammered. Nicolai delivered us to our hotel room where Robin and I literally laughed ourselves to sleep.

Early in the evening we were awakened by the noise of people in front of the hotel, making their way to the concert hall. We looked at the clock and realized that in ten minutes Seiji Ozawa would walk out on stage and do his dance that would launch the San Francisco Symphony's performance. Instantly we went from stupor to trooper, there was no time to be hung over. We ran across the street to the concert hall, found our wardrobe trunk, changed into concert dress and checked to see if all the instruments we needed for the concert were in place. Whew! Deep Breath. The music began and I was embraced by the infectious Russian love of music. (This wonderful city had charmed me in 1962 and now, eleven years later, this feeling was enhanced by more experience and a deeper understanding of its extraordinary history. During World War II Dimitri Shostakovich wrote his Symphony No. 7, *The Leningrad*. It was written during the seige of Leningrad in the winter of 1941-42. The music was motivated by the ruthless treatment of the Russian people that was begun by Stalin and that Hitler's troups were trying to complete. Shostakovich captured the feelings, the suffering, the deep yearnings, the social mood, in the moment of the music. I can only imagine the collective spirit at the performances of this music—the defiance of injustice—the proud Russian spirit singing out to meet the challenges of life.)

The next afternoon Robin and I again walked across the street from our hotel to the concert hall. The place seemed empty. Robin took his snare drum to the conductor's podium and began to play the snare drum part from Shostakovich's Leningrad Symphony. The drum plays a repetitive rhythm that provides the pulse and momentum of an entire movement in the music. I closed my eyes and history began to wash over me. All of a sudden I began to hear men's voices singing the trombone and trumpet parts to the music. Robin continued to play with an intensity that only he was capable of, and the voices grew louder and louder. I opened my eyes and saw two older men standing in the center of the stage singing their hearts out. When the music ended Robin and I joined them at center stage. Through bits of Russian, German, and English we discovered that these two men had been the principal trombone and principal trumpet of the Leningrad Philharmonic Orchestra in 1941 and actually experienced the siege of the city and many performances of this music. They were crying; we all embraced and the tears flowed. They had obviously been enjoying some vodka somewhere in the building when they heard Robin's call to arms. This shared understanding led to more tears and hugs. One of the men shouted "Encore!" and Robin made his way to the drum and began the incessant rhythm. One more time through all the hot brass licks of the music, and we found ourselves holding each other again—confirming and celebrating the ancient path that music has woven through the warp and weft of the human experience.

JAPAN

Professional collaborations, devotion to music, and strong personal friendships with Seiji Ozawa and Toru Takemitsu drew me quite naturally into frequent experiences with and a deep appreciation for the Japanese people and their rich culture. With my first visit to Japan in 1969 I experienced an immediate intuitive affinity, creating a sense of being at home

Coincidentally, inspired by *The Three Pillars of Zen* by Roshi Philip Kapleau, the path of my spiritual journey had arrived at an exploration of the Zen Buddhist tradition as practiced in Japan and at the Rochester Zen Center, which had been established by Roshi Kapleau after fourteen years of study and practice in Japan. When interest in Buddhism began to spread from the Indian subcontinent north through southeast Asia into China, it had a close encounter with an already well-established Taoist tradition. The influence of that interaction led to Chan Buddhism in China and consequently Zen Buddhism in Japan. I was already familiar with the Taoist classic, the *Tao Te Ching*, attributed to Lao Tzu; when beginning to read the classics of the Chan and the Zen traditions, I found so many similarities between Taoism and Zen that there seemed to be a unison of essence in the two traditions. All of this has been so clearly and beautifully explored in the work of Ray Grigg—*The Tao of Zen*, and the brilliant writings of Deng Ming-Dao, which present the Taoist tradition in a sensitive, contemporary, relevant way.

After thirty years of visits, I have come to see that I always leave Japan healthier in body, mind, and spirit, than when I arrived, inspired to be more productive, more creative, and more attentive.

Over the past ten years I've been building stone walls and using stone in landscape and gardening projects. Stones have become my advisors and are teaching me about the importance of work. Give me a pile of stones and I become a child. Singing as I work, while becoming lost in a wonderful world of building something. Learning to read stone so it will tell you where and how it would like to be placed is learning to accept nature as it is and following its ways.

The Japanese gardening traditions bring centuries of experience and insight to the observation of nature and have universal applications to any creative process:

Mono no aware—sensitivity towards things—emotional quality of things—rocks, flowers, trees—sensitive to their sensitivity.

Kohan ni shitagau—following the request. It's important to follow the request of what already exists on the garden site.

Yohaku no bi—less is more—the beauty of empty space (silence-stillness), allowing for the imagination of the beholder.

Wabi—restraint and poverty—simple and modest.

Amakusa

Five thirty a.m. The warm haze of a summer morning awaits the sun's rays to release its colors. Mika arrives at Shinwaso Ryokan and we make our way to Houshoji Temple. I've already been up since 4:30 anticipating the experience. Wako Murakami, the head monk, has invited me to join him in waking the town by ringing the huge temple bell eighteen times. This bell is so massive that the piece of wood used to strike it is a log eight inches in diameter and five feet long, suspended at both ends from ropes that allow it to swing freely so it can strike the bell and get the massive metal to vibrate. What a sound! With Wako's first ring, the town is engulfed in the most powerful bell sound I have ever experienced. Standing at the source, there is only sound. Wako bows a deep *gassho* to the bell, and we listen to the long sustain ring out. Taking the rope attached to the log, I swing it back and forth to feel its weight. Swinging it back as far as possible, I direct it to the beating spot on the bell and await the wash of sound that would engulf the neighborhood. Following Wako's example, I bowed and listened. This was the largest mass of metal I had ever touched with the goal of getting it to ring. After my first shot I knew (as always) there was room for improvement. How to increase the chi in my stroke? By relaxing and deepening the respiration, the sound of each successive touch of the log to the bell became richer. Wako and I were alternating, so I had his experienced example to inspire me.

After this cosmic sunrise serenade, we entered the temple and went to Wako's living quarters where his wife, Yukimi, served us fresh figs warmed in plum wine, along with some green tea. Wako proceeded to tell me that our reverence for the decay of the bell sound had resulted in the longest wake-up call in recent memory.

Mika introduced me to Wako at a concert we were playing together in Nagasaki. I was struck by his genuineness and we established an instant friendship.

Mika Yoshida is a marimbist who makes her home on the island of Amakusa, a small island about fifty minutes by boat south of Kumamoto. Mika plays with a passion and enthusiasm that charms her audiences. She's the cultural ambassador of Amakusa and is rapidly establishing her international career as a powerful musician. Many collaborative concerts with Mika since 1995 have enriched my life, as I have been welcomed into her family and circle of friends in Hondo City.

During the summer of 2001 I spent a month participating in the Amakusa Ceramics Festival, working with artists at the Maruo Ceramic Studio in Hondo City, developing bells and percussion instruments made from clay.

There is a real warmth in the people of Amakusa that has welcomed me, touched my heart, and made me feel at home.

Nine Japanese Word-Guides

Shizen Tai: Spontaneity
> Dance to the ceaseless changes of life. Consistency is the hobgoblin of a narrow mind.

Wa: Harmony
> United in Accordance

Onwa: Softness
> Through gentleness the mind becomes clear—Loving Touch—Receptive

Heisei: Balance
> See many perspectives—Attach importance to none—Moderation—Sharing

Nintai: Patience
> Rooted in wholeness—patience changes fear into love—accepting

Mushin: Selflessness
> The joy of living begins by giving yourself away. The servant of the Music.

Ishin: Oneness
> Unification—Being There

Ku Kyo: Emptiness
> Accepting the sublime tranquillity of repose—clear reflection in tranquillity

Mu: Nothingness

Ascetic Aesthetics
Following the sound to now

Attentiveness in Buddhist practice is often enhanced by the use of sound. Both Chan and Zen traditions have developed bells that have a very long sustain to their sound. Once the bell is set vibrating it will ring on its own for more than two minutes. In a quiet environment it really tunes the being.

While touring Japan in 1975 with the San Francisco Symphony Orchestra I had the opportunity to introduce many friends in the orchestra to these amazing bells. In a period of three days in Kyoto many of the musicians had purchased bells. One evening six of us gathered in my hotel room for the purpose of a moment musicale with the new bells, and soon we discovered that the acoustic space was much too small. We needed a more expansive venue for our performance. Someone suggested the stairwells at either end of the corridor, so the six of us divided up into two groups of three in each stairwell with each player on a different floor. The results were magnificent. The cavernous stairwells responded like a cathedral of stairwells to the stars. The bells were enhanced by the resonant acoustics and inspired vocalizations that were otherworldly. In short order the hotel security was all over us, but to our surprise they did not stop us but sat in with us and joined the music by chanting and playing the bells. It was a magic creative moment for a group of musicians and security officers finding a harmony together by sharing sound.

CHINA

February 1978: Beijing, China, at the very end of the cultural revolution and the trial of the Gang of Four. The Toronto Symphony had just arrived after several concerts in Japan. Andrew Davis was conducting, and contralto Maureen Forrester had joined the TSO for our series of concerts in Beijing, Shanghai, and Kwongchow. The air was very cold and filled with red dust blowing in from the deserts of Mongolia. My mind was filled with curiosity and anticipation of the adventure that was unfolding. It's amazing that even after years of travel, youthful energy, enthusiasm and curiosity still blossom at the opportunity to explore a new culture and look at life in a new way.

In 1978 the Chinese people were not used to tourists, and wandering in the city could be problematic. If you stopped to observe something or walked into a shop you would immediately draw a crowd and your freedom to wander was curtailed by a curious group of people. Upon arrival in Beijing I was approached by John Fraser, then head of the China desk for the Toronto Globe and Mail. He asked if I would like to join him and Maureen on a visit to the Forbidden City. We arrived at our destination and began walking toward the main entrance when Maureen and I were drawn to an inscription on a wall. As we approached the wall a crowd began to gather, and very soon we were trapped against the wall by several hundred people pushing forward to see what was happening. I turned to Maureen, wondering how we might escape from this prison of curiosity. She turned toward the people, threw open her arms and began singing. The crowd fell back, I offered my arm, she took it and continued to sing. As we took a step forward a path opened up; I felt like I was on stage at the Met. We strolled through the crowd as Maureen parted the gathering of people with the power of song. It was one of the most powerful performances I've ever observed and from the best seat in the house. Over twenty years later I still feel a thrill race up my spine when I remember the experience.

Looking for new sounds was one of my major preoccupations during the TSO tour of China. For thousands of years the Chinese culture has practiced the art of creating bells, gongs, cymbals, drums, and many other amazing sources of sound. Every city had its own unique sense of sound and craftsmanship. I took two empty trunks with me on the tour in anticipation of expanding my palette of sonorities. Given John Fraser's knowledge of Beijing, I knew exactly were to go in our first city in China. Every instrument I tried was a new horizon in sound. (Now I'm the kind of guy who's never had a bad meal, and I'm not sure if that comes from a love of eating, a good appetite, or something lacking in my ability to discriminate.) The fact that none of the instruments had any prices on them did not deter me, and when I discovered that all of the metallic cymbals and gongs were sold by weight, I began creating piles of sounds on the large scales in the shop. I became a child turned loose in a toy shop, my only limit being how much I could transport to the hotel.

Our stage manager, Reg Taylor, helped put a rack together so I could suspend many of the new instruments and surprise Andrew and Maureen when we rehearsed a piece of Chinese music she was singing with the orchestra. I was able to improvise and add some more authentic sounds to the arrangement for Western symphony orchestra.

By now the word was out and all the music shops in Beijing were loaded with orchestra members looking for new sounds.

This made shopping very difficult. I was forced to take a new tack. I did some advance research to locate the music shops in Shanghai and Kwongchow. Since our luggage was taken care of by the orchestra, when we arrived in each city I would take a taxi directly from the airport to the music shop, thus enabling me to explore the instruments in a calm, quiet environment, then arrive at the hotel as the orchestra personnel of one hundred plus were just finishing their check-in procedure.

During our stay in China, local tuba players were coming out of the closet and returning to their positions in symphony orchestras from which they had all been banished during the cultural revolution. The Chinese believed that low notes came from the devil.

One of the most moving experiences of our tour of China took place in Beijing. At the end of one of our rehearsals the members of the Toronto Symphony were asked to sit in the audience seats and listen to the performance of a Chinese musician. His story was a sad and heroic tale. At the beginning of the cultural revolution his violin was taken away from him and destroyed because he was practicing Western music, and he was banished to an island. On the island he secretly built his own violin and continued to practice until he had the opportunity to return home. This man poured his heart out to us. The real human emotion and empathy in that concert hall was beyond description.

How can anyone presume to know how someone else should live. . .

I'm not pointing my finger at the Chinese here. We all have our rules, the tools of control. To impose an order creates disorder. Humanity in its grandest dreams and schemes has never come close to the splendor of the natural order of things.

Blame does not allow wounds to heal—forgiveness does. The world will always need a good dose of cooperation.

The possibility of compromise is continually frustrated by orthodox belief systems designed for societies thousands of years ago.

> Prophets lead to profits—for disciples—
>   reaping a living from the lost and found.
> Belief uses and then refuses to understand Now.
>
> It's not what we don't know that's a problem.
> It's what we think we know for sure that obscures the way.

❖

Is not the reconciliation of differences the real exercise of life?

—Toru Takemitsu

❖

Earth Provides
—Karachi, Pakistan, 1985—

The earth provides so much—enough for all
let's share it—work together—hear its call
Life's so dear—to waste on fear
how can anyone presume to know
    how someone else should live
we're the only living things that think we know
    and when we see we're wrong
        that's when we grow
how can anyone presume to know
    how someone else should live
we're the only living things that think we know
    and when we see we're wrong
        that's when we grow
how can anyone presume to know

In the early 1980s while Jean and I were managing the business aspects of Nexus, our work culminated in a four-month world tour that began in China, so in May of 1984 I found myself once again in Beijing. Recalling some experiences with the TSO in 1978 I had some idea of what would be expected in terms of protocol at official events. I knew that I would be required to address our hosts, ministers of culture and other officials of the government of China, the Canadian Ambassador and his family and staff, and most frequently the audiences at our concerts and workshops. I thought that it would be good if I could learn to speak some Chinese; so I got together with Stephen Lee, one of Russell Hartenberger's students at the University of Toronto. Stephen had grown up in Hong Kong and had immigrated to Canada to pursue his studies. I suggested that we develop one paragraph that would work as a greeting, describing where Nexus was from and why we were in China, and another paragraph that would serve to end a speech or concert showing appreciation, ending with "Peace be with you." Stephen wrote it all out phonetically and then coached me in all the musical inflections that are so meaningful in the Chinese language. The basic text was in Mandarin, with a few minor adjustments for the different cities.

I arrived in Beijing three days before Jean and Nexus in order to take care of final arrangements, including the arrival of our twenty-five trunks of instruments. I had lots of time to practice my Chinese phrases and get some feedback from the official translator, Wang Chou, who was assigned to Nexus. Jet lag had me ready to roll by four a.m., so every morning I walked from the hotel to the Temple of Heaven and through the grounds and gardens around the Temple, reciting my two paragraphs of Chinese over and over again, sometimes out loud and sometimes to myself.

In the wee hours of the morning the grounds of the Temple of Heaven were a living ballet of Chinese culture, with many different groups of people stretching and flowing in unison, following the example of their teachers. Many individuals danced alone with their own variations on a theme by Tai Chi and Chi Gung. Some folks embraced trees while others greeted the rising sun. Groups of older men gathered under the trees where they could hang the small bamboo bird cages they brought from their homes, sharing their interest in their aviary friends and delighting in their songs. Remembering the admonition of Roshi Kapleau emphasizing practice, I found myself walking very slowly with a smooth deliberate step, the left hand wrapped around the right fist, both held against the chest. Practicing Kinnin, a walking meditation, the phrase, "Peace be with you," (in Chinese of course, "Yuan Hoaping

Changyu Ni Men, Zai I Chi") became a mantra, sometimes internalized but often vocalized in order to practice the inflections that were so unusual for the traditional habit patterns of my speech.

I knew I faced a challenge in familiarizing the guys in Nexus with the sound of my speaking Chinese. I couldn't handle the possibility of someone losing it at the welcome banquet, so I practiced my Chinese phrases on them in the van on the way to the banquet.

According to the traditional order of things, our Chinese hosts would welcome us and propose a series of toasts during the first course of appetizers, then it would be my turn to respond in kind with greetings from Nexus and the people of Canada. I had my thoughts organized and memorized, beginning in Chinese, continuing in English with pauses so that Wang Chou could translate, then finishing up in Chinese. The plan seemed solid, but like so many things in life they didn't unfold as I thought they would. Our host, Mr. Hu Shu-Shun from the China Performing Arts Agency, was an old hand at welcome banquets and a very outgoing man who loved to make toasts. There was plenty of great Chinese beer, but all the toasts were made with mao tai. Now we're talkin' some pretty strong liquor here. They drink it in tiny glasses, which is an indication out in front that we're dealing with some toxic stuff. When you pour it into the glass it emits a smoky vapor. I've never been much of a juice head, but Mr. Hu had a real buzz for mao tai, and by the time we were just half way through the appetizers, we had already thrown back five hits of this stuff. The doubts began to creep in as I wondered if I would be able to remember my speech, speak clearly, and—bottom line—could I stand up? My heart was pounding in my chest like the bass drum part in the *Pines of Rome*. I had never felt this kind of angst in my life. I took a long, slow, deep breath, grabbed Wang Chou by the hand, stood up and launched into my speech before Mr. Hu found another opportunity to raise his glass. The applause after the opening paragraph was long enough to allow for another slow deep breath, and all the pauses for Wang Chou to translate my English gave me more chances to deepen my respiration and slow down the drum that was pounding away in my chest. As I began the final section of the speech I could see light at the end of the tunnel, segued right into a toast to the universal language of music, and oozed into my chair to receive the next blast of mao tai.

Nexus was the first Western percussion ensemble to tour China and most of our music was new for the audience. Traditional audience behavior challenged us at first, but we adjusted. It is not uncommon for Chinese audiences to talk during performances, discussing the music, the price of rice, the weather, who knows? We had to raise the volume levels of some of our more gentle repertoire like Takemitsu's "Rain Tree," losing the subtle end of dynamics. But the freedom the Chinese people felt to express themselves during performance made for some interesting interactions twixt musicians and audience. "Music for Pieces of Wood," by the American composer Steve Reich, is written for five pairs of tuned claves. The piece is organized in three sections, with each section containing a different rhythmic pattern with a different rhythmic feel. With each change in the piece came an audience response in the form of a wave of conversation that began in the front of the auditorium and worked its way to the rear of the hall, gradually fading into more attentive listening until the next change in the piece when the process would be repeated. An amazing ebb and flow between music and audience.

The hit of our concerts in China was a composition of Bill Cahn's, "The Birds." Hundreds of bird whistles and bird calls woven into a texture of percussion sounds touched the Chinese people in a genuine way, and they responded with enthusiasm.

Wanting Less

The greatest evil : wanting more
 The worst luck : discontent
  To know enough's enough is enough to know.

—Lao Tzu
(trans. Ursula K. Le Guin)

The Symphony Orchestra

Being a member of a symphony orchestra is an extraordinary experience. Taking part in the re-creation of music from the imaginations of composers of the last three hundred years is a wonderful journey, by sound, through the shapes, forms, colors, tensions, apprehensions, suspensions, visions, revisions, dreams, extremes, and moonbeams of the sublime juice of creativity. Inspired by life, a lover, all rife, then hover to discover a new way of saying the same old thing. Or is it the same old way of saying something new?—Nowness is Newness.

A glorious experience—being—part of it all

Playing timpani in an orchestra brings one to the very heart of the matter. The very heartbeat of the music is where the timpani part is often found. The kettledrums are usually set up at the rear of the orchestra, center stage, so the timpanist has a great view of the entire orchestra, audience, and concert hall— the big picture —

>through eyes and ears
>nose and throat
>dancing limbs
>in an old tail coat
>the realm of Awe
>was always near
>and all I had to do
>was Hear—Don't Listen
>Listen—Don't Hear

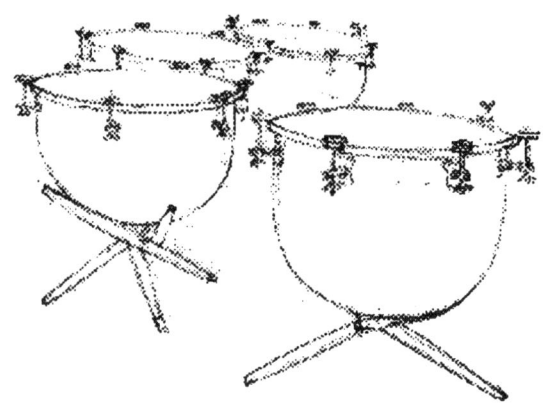

Given the physical presence of the large copper bowls that surround the player, timpanists are required to move around in order to play the part, so it is acceptable for the players to include dance in their approach to the drums. Continuous motion conserves energy. Starting and stopping both deal with inertia and demand more energy to overcome the inertia. Stopping and starting can also create tension that blocks the flow of energy. Keep it movin'! Fill your space with grace. We need a constant flow of chi throughout the body to bring vitality to the music. Tai Chi is the marriage of movement and meditation, and the practice of Tai Chi brings a vitality and a consistent concentrated flow to the dance of life.

Often in the orchestral repertoire the timpanist will have many places in the music where there is no part to play, but there is a need to keep in touch with the music so you know when to make your next entrance. The traditional way of maintaining an awareness of your place in the flow of the music is by counting measures of rest. For example, if each measure has four beats and there are sixty-three measures rest, the count would be one-two-three-four, two-two-three-four, three-two-three-four, four-two-three-four, etc., all the way to sixty-three-two-three-four, leading into the next entrance. Often the mind wanders from the counting process—one's attention is drawn in by the music or is distracted by unwanted thoughts that creep on to the horizon of consciousness, or is just lost in a reverie in the garden of sentimental memories. With experience one learns to trust the re-emergence of the counting process when it happens. For example, one might be transfixed by a beautiful melody from the oboe or be thinking about the lovely smile on the lady in the second row of the balcony, when out of the depths comes forty-seven-two-three-four. When I began meditating I began by following the breath and counting the in and out cycles of breathing. The same experience of the counting process submerging and reappearing occurred, and I began to realize the importance of deepening the respiration, developing attentiveness, and trusting the intuitive. Practice can develop all of these functions of being. The release of tension, the reduction of stress, the quieting of the mind are all results of the practice of meditation and deepened respiration.

From time to time the orchestra program will include music in which your instrument is not needed for an entire movement, so counting measures can be suspended and a more centered approach to the practice of meditation can be undertaken. Imagine sitting on stage with 90-100 musicians, sometimes a choir of 50-200 singers, being still, deepening the breathing, and losing yourself in it all. Glorious!

These moments of blissful repose also present an opportunity to build up chi or prana, vital energy to help meet the (often rigorous) demands of the music. Bringing one's attention to the hara (the area just below the navel), breathing in and out slowly and fully, and visualizing the hara as your access to the universal energy of the music, can be helpful in accessing the strength that is needed to realize some of the repertoire, and can also be helpful in keeping the body balanced amidst the movements of the dance of performance. The physical demands of playing in a symphony orchestra can be substantial. If you think otherwise, take a shot at Beethoven's Ninth Symphony, the Verdi Requiem, any symphony by Sibelius, or any opera by Richard Strauss. Muscle power is not the answer to a big beautiful sound. Everything I know about sound is in my ears. The influence of touch on the quality of the sound has more to do with the character of the musician than with his or her physical traits.

Reach out and touch someone. Music is not an exercise, indifference sucks. Every sound you create is precious and meaningful. If you don't love what you're doing—don't do it! Work without joy will kill you and bore your audience to sleep or to the exit. Perception determines communication. Hear the whole band and share that perception with the audience. Often in orchestra rehearsals I would concentrate my focus on one voice in the music, particularly if the part I was about to play interacted in some way with that voice. For example, if the cellos had a line I was about to interact with I would focus on them intently and, invariably, as I entered with my part some of the cellists would look in my direction and confirm the communication. Eventually it became clear to me that what is perceived is what is shared. We are what we experience, the unison confirms this. Unity is what is given. Technique, methods, style, are tools. Music is about life and communication. Just surrender—to the sound—the unison has so much to give.

At this point in my life, one of the challenges I face is to keep music precious so that performance is enthusiastic and joyful. Sincerity and spontaneity bring a preciousness to music. Change: new sounds, new music, new instruments, embraced with an openness to explore, generate the enthusiasm that comes with discovery. I don't listen to music as much as I used to, and I enjoy periods where there is no performance or music in my daily routine. When cooking food, the best sauce is hunger. Age and experience temper passion and teach us about balance and moderation in our life.

Is there too much music in our daily lives? Yes—too much of anything creates apathy—we learn to shut it out—take it for granted. Music is not a background exercise to encourage shopping in stores or digestion in restaurants or to relieve boredom in elevators, airplanes and doctors' waiting rooms. Music is a nourishing experience in our lives, a healing force to be savored single-mindedly. When shopping—only shop. When eating—only eat. When waiting—only wait, an opportunity for stillness. When driving—only drive. When listening—only listen!

In the 1970s Toru Takemitsu was asked to write some music to be played for the shoppers at the Seibu department stores in Japan. The reaction was unexpected: the shoppers stopped shopping and just listened to the music! Sales decreased, so the music was removed. Score one for listening!

Stress

The question I am most frequently asked by students and professional colleagues alike is how do I deal with stress?

First of all, don't take anything personally. Toward the end of his career Maestro William Steinberg came to conduct the Toronto Symphony. He was very old and frail and very wise. At one point in the rehearsal he turned to one of the musicians and made a comment about how his part related to the music. Upon receiving these comments from the Maestro the musician became very nervous and befuddled. Steinberg was aware that his comments had upset the musician, so he stood in silence for a moment then said, "Composer's wrong, conductor's wrong, performer's wrong, we're all wrong! OK?" The whole orchestra laughed and the tension dissolved instantly. We need to be able to laugh at it all, so don't take life so personally and don't take life so seriously. Laughter is the best medicine.

Next, do what you love to do. If you don't enjoy what you're doing, find something that you love to do and you will find happiness and bring joy to others.

Staying physically relaxed is essential in dealing with stress. It's easy for drummers to dance when they play. Continuous motion can make movement seem effortless, and at the very core of physical performance on any instrument is a deep, full, relaxed breath. The breath is our link between the mind and the body.

Slow it down. Slow it all down. Don't be in a hurry. Think slow to play fast. The tempo of contemporary urban life is stressful and urgent. Technology has created an unhealthy demand for instant results and instant responses. What goes up must come down. Hard work must be balanced by rest. What goes fast must go slow. Everything must rest—body, mind, spirit. Everything must work—body, mind, spirit. Balance and moderation are the keys to health. The body is designed by nature to find its nutrients from a wide variety of sources, and so it is with mind and spirit.

Many musicians today are becoming wired to pharmaceuticals in an attempt to deal with nervousness and stress during performance. Where does nervousness come from? What are the roots of stress? Inquire into this. Drugs of any kind, including alcohol, can confer momentary vacations from concern, changes of consciousness, and occasional perceptions of altered sensitivities; but they also bring about weakened mental and physical conditions. Long-term use brings long-term debilitating effects. **Tune yourself,** as well as your instrument. Quiet the mind, deepen the respiration, practice relaxation, and embrace the fact that in life there is nothing like being real. Reality offers the insight and power of nowness.

Nicotine, caffeine, remember the rush? The release of adrenaline, a stress hormone. Alcohol, drugs, often used to tranquilize, can acerbate anxiety and irritability. Refined sugar creates blood sugar swings that make it more difficult to manage stress. Just a few of the things that I've loved and embraced passionately in my life and have come to see, through real life experience, that they mess me up. I'm not advocating abstinence here. Life is to be experienced, all of it, but we must be open to and be able to read and respond to our body's reaction to what we consume; and our mind's response to what we ingest; and our spirit's response to how we live. You are the pilot of your ship—you, not your doctor, not your lawyer, not your preacher, not your financial advisor. What comes out of us is made up of what we put in. Take an interest in what you ingest.

Moderation and balance are the key.

Real Being — Listen! — Simply Perceive — don't question what you hear — Go with it! Trust your perceptions and let the music be the leader. If what you hear is ambiguous, clarify it (play à la referee). But remember, it's not your personal authority or power you're reinforcing, but the authority of the music as it unfolds.

Be gentle with yourself. Recognize mistakes, and then forget them. There's no future in guilt. Be free to fail, there are no winners, we are all beginners.

In 1964 I received an unsigned letter saying:
"Mind the Wind and lose yourself among its Smile."

The thought inspired the following song:

Wind Song
—Norland, 1972—

The joy of living
begins—by giving yourself a-way
be free to fail
there are no winners
we are all beginners
we've forgotten to forgive
freedom lies inside
locked up by debt and pride
let go of what we think should be
and give our souls a ride
just like to lose this idea
I have of myself
just like to lose this idea
I have of myself

World Drums

World drum festivals have given me an extended family. Since 1984 it has been my great fortune to direct and participate in many different World Drums' productions, bringing together musicians from many nations around the globe. Collaborating with more than five hundred artists has provided opportunities to experience first hand the extraordinary diversity that exists in the art of drumming and to discover those things that link us together along this ancient path called music. There are those who would say we should stay within our own traditions and be consistent and loyal to our own roots and cultural ways. Tradition can be a cruel padlock, and consistency demands that we stay as ignorant today as we were last week. Our roots are in this vast universe that includes, supports, sustains, inspires, and transforms us.

The seeds of the world drum dream began to sprout in late December and early January of 1961, in the middle of the Eastman Philharmonia's three-month tour of Europe, the Middle East, and what was then the Soviet Union. Christmas was spent on the island of Cyprus. The orchestra stayed at the Ledra Palace Hotel in the city of Nicosia in the center of the island, near the demarcation line that went from east to west dividing the island between the Greek Cypriots to the south and the Turkish Cypriots to the north. The tension between the two cultures was palpable and stressful. It was interesting that the musicians, instruments, and musical influences in the house band at the hotel represented both Greek and Turkish cultures as well as European, North American, and Arabic traditions.

From Cyprus we flew to Aleppo Syria; apparently the government had gone through a recent change and we were guilty of performing the wrong national anthem. There were some disturbances in the concert hall lobby in response to our mistake, but the audience settled down as we continued with the concert.

This was my first journey to the ancient heart of an Arab-Islamic culture. The traditions were both challenging and charming. The people, music, design concepts, carpets, the geometry of the architecture, and the food, all seduced me completely. The sublime poetry teased my young years into a glimpse of the wisdom of the Sufi Mystics. Challenges came from the Souk, the way of business-bargaining, being lost in the maze of shops and stalls, different body language, veiled women, the tradition of no physical contact between men and women in public—this was all new to me. From Syria we flew to Egypt. In Cairo we performed in the Opera House where Verdi's opera *Aida* was premiered. It's amazing how the spirit of a concert hall reaches out and touches you, its history becoming part of you. After New Year's Eve celebrations in Alexandria we were off to Beirut.

Several times our bus was stopped and boarded by soldiers with machine guns, searching, in absolute silence. It's interesting, the respect a weapon commands, and how very quiet a bus load of young musicians can be when they're attentive. Welcome to the Holy Lands! The dialogue of Moslems, Christians and Jews. The Palestinian refuge settlements we passed through, already twelve years old, were a crime against humanity, an experience that I will never forget. In all my travels through the Middle East the holy lands have taught me that all lands are holy, and ancient traditions are not finding solutions for today's challenges.

At a reception after our concert in Beirut I had a new experience, making music with musicians performing on instruments from other cultures: A Lebanese trio playing an *oud*, a *ney*, and a *dombek*; a man from India playing tabla; and I was playing bongos. Tabla, bongos, dombek—three hand drums, three very different cultures working together in harmony and with great joy. The source of our union was MUSIC. The dream of bringing drummers together from all over the world began to take shape in my imagination.

John Cripton, the Canadian entrepreneur-dreamer extraordinaire, was the producer of the Toronto International Festival in 1984, and he came to the rescue of my world drum dream with a resounding Yes, let's do it! The event was called Supercussion. It took place in Toronto's Roy Thomson Hall and brought together artists and music from Asia, Africa, Europe, and North and South America. Sixteen musicians came together to share their traditions: Brian Leonard Barlow from Toronto, Samul Nori from Korea, Sharda Sahai from Banares, India, Abraham Adzenyah from Ghana, Repercussion from Montreal, and Nexus from Toronto. The concert was a joy to put together and was very successful. It was well-documented by film maker John McGreevy. I knew this concept was a natural, and John Cripton made sure that the executive producer of the cultural programs for Expo 86 in Vancouver, Ann Farris, was aware of the World Drums Dream. When Ann asked if I would like to organize and direct a large World Drum Festival on a global scale, I exploded instantly—YES! YES! YES!—I was certain it would work.

After setting some logistical parameters (budget, size, when, how long, venues), we set to work to realize the dream. I began a list of the artists I hoped could and would be able to participate. Sal Ferreras, an amazing musician who grew up in San Juan, Puerto Rico, and Caracas, Venezuela, joined the dream as assistant director. Sal makes his home in Vancouver and has been an essential part of all the World Drum Festivals

I've had the good fortune to realize. Sal's musical talents and sensitivities are as natural as his easy going character. He has that rare chameleon quality found in some great performers that allows them to lose themselves in the music and take on the very spirit of the moment. A map of the world helped us to locate the areas requiring some search and research. Letters were sent to all countries participating in Expo, explaining our plans and asking for their support and advice. Journeys were planned to seek out talented musicians from those parts of the world where I had no previous experience with the musical culture.

From early spring of 1985 to the summer of 1986 I traveled and dreamed of a thousand ways to fill the days of a two-week festival of the drums of the world. How to plan the finale remained a big question in my mind, in light of the fact that nothing had ever turned out the way I had planned. Let it be! Shit Happens—trusting the intuitive, knowing that it would work began to nibble away at the perimeters of the question, reducing it to manageable proportions. The unknown always presents challenges and insights as to how to proceed.

Istanbul

In May of 1985, while searching for musicians for the festival, I found myself in the city of minarets. The art of the carpet had touched me, and my passionate response had sent my spending reeling. Jean had threatened the removal of all credit cards on this journey if I did not restrain my desire to acquire. Carpet shops abound in the great city of Istanbul, and emerging from the 1947 Desoto stretch "taxhi" I was seduced by the first carpet shop I encountered. After several hours of losing myself in carpets I confided in the owner of the shop the real purpose of my visit to Turkey. Once he understood my quest for drums and drummers he called for Gurhan, one of his assistants. Gurhan K. Sodan was an artist-writer who supported his creative calling by working in the carpet shop. He knew the artistic community in the city and proceeded to give me the royal tour. We began in a part of the city where we found many traditional music shops. Walking down the narrow street I found myself surrounded by tiny establishments that serviced the musicians of Istanbul. Their windows were filled with all the traditional string, wind, and percussion instruments that are part of the classical, folk, and popular musics of Turkey.

The *darabuka* is one of the traditional hand drums of Turkey, the Balkan countries, and most of the Islamic cultures of North Africa, from Egypt west to Morocco. *Dara* is a generic term for drum, and *buka* is an onomatopoetic description of the sounds of the instrument. *Bu* represents the low fundamental tone of the drum, and *ka* describes the higher sounds that come from playing on the rim of the drum. In Syria, Lebanon, and Israel, a similar drum is called a *dombek*; *dom* being the low sound and *bek* being the high rim sounds.

The street of musical instrument shops in Istanbul was on a hilly slope, offering a panorama, and for a moment I lost myself in the big picture—ancient traditions, centuries of Christian and Islamic evolution, crossroads of cultures and empires, the amazing architectural landscape punctuated by a sea of minarets dancing on the horizon.

The afternoon sun reflected off of a large brass object in one of the shop windows. It was surrounded by string instruments—ouds, kanuns, and many more that I was not familiar with. As I approached the window the sun's glare subsided and revealed the largest, most intricately engraved darabuka I'd ever seen. Entering the tiny shop I inquired about the drum in the window. The proprietor didn't seem anxious to talk about the instrument. I persisted and asked if I could look at it. He was still reluctant to retrieve the drum from the window. After pleading with him for some time he finally gave in and approached the window. Ten minutes passed as he carefully removed all the string instruments from the window display and found safe places to put them in the tiny shop before he could remove the drum from its place in the center of the display. He handed it to me and I sat in the only chair in the shop and laid the big drum across my lap. I paused for a moment, looking at the drum, knowing it was a monster; the anticipation within me was reaching epic proportions. Raising my right hand, and praying to the Great God of Touch to guide it to the sweet spot that would release the big bottom Bu of the Buka, I touched the drum near the center of the drumhead with a moderate amount of energy and was transfixed by the mellowest, longest, and lowest fundamental I had ever heard from a hand drum. The entire shop responded with sympathetic vibrations. I looked at the shopkeeper with the contented smile of a pilgrim who had found the source of the pilgrimage, and said "MY drum!" The proprietor became very excited and insisted that he was not about to sell me my drum. Not for sale, not for sale he shouted. My drum, my drum, I replied. There came an awkward silence that I ended by asking the man if he was a musician. He said he was and explained that he played the oud. I looked him right in the eye and said then you must understand that I have found my instrument. Noticing his resistance weakening I felt that I was reaching him. Our dialogue continued for an eternity as I tried to persuade him to sell the drum. Falling to my knees I embraced the darabuka and fixed my gaze on the proprietor and declared once more that I had found my instrument and now I must live with it and learn from it and go where it would take me. His expression softened and I knew once more that I had reached him, but still he offered no response. Finally I offered to give him anything he wanted in return for the drum. At that his eyes opened wide, and the matter was quickly resolved.

Returning to the carpet shop I thanked Gurhan for his assistance in bringing this new inspiring sound source into my life, and quickly established myself in one of the upstairs showrooms where I could explore the darabuka and the carpets simultaneously. It was a warm day in May and the windows were open, bringing the sounds of the street and market into the room. Cities—cultures—carpets—all have rhythms. I was transported by the sounds from the drum. Weaving my way through the new environment of visual patterns and aural stimuli, I entered into a paradise of exploration and lost myself in this Turkish Delight. A powerful haunting voice entered through the window, quieting the sounds of the street momentarily. It was the call to prayer from a nearby mosque. The drum fell silent, a stillness set in and my gaze became fixed on a carpet. Perceiving the inward journey of the spiritual path, I was reminded by the muzziem of the blessings of sound. What a wonderful tool this music is, this magic carpet of sounds that leads us to ourselves.

Pakistan

From Istanbul I went to Pakistan, where one hot day (114°F) I found myself in Islamabad at a cultural center where artists lived and worked together. Traveling and looking for participants for the World Drum Festival had quickly revealed my first major challenge: I wanted to invite everyone. One musician in particular at the cultural center in Islamabad touched me very deeply. He played an instrument he called a *chimta*. Picture a flat strip of steel about six feet long, one inch wide, and about one-sixteenth-of-an-inch thick, tapered to a point at each end. Bend the strip of steel at the centre to form a tweezers about three feet long. A brass ring at the closed end of the tweezers is held in the right hand in such a way as to allow the player to tap the brass ring against the steel strip. The left hand holds the opened end of the tweezers' tips between thumb and fingers in order to open and close the tweezers. Sounds pretty simple. Well, this artist drew a symphony out of this chimta, accompanying his vocalizations and dance. I asked him how he learned to play the chimta and his reply was clear and simple: "My master told me—you must study with the chimta, it will teach you everything you need to know."

From Islamabad I traveled south to Lahore, the great cultural capital of the ancient Mogul culture. Ramadan was providing many days of solitude, as most sources of food and culture were closed from dawn to dusk. It's wonderful how being alone can facilitate the journey within. The exploration of Being; seeing and feeling our relatedness, experiencing the organic wholeness of the Universe—The Source. The imagination responds with its celebration of and longing for unification. My days were spent writing songs.

Toccare

for Jean

—Lahore, Pakistan, 1985—

Touch is such
oh so much
how I love to hold you
and when you touch me
oh - so - healing
revealing
the way your voice embraces me
and keeps my fears away
I love you
more than I can say
yes—I love you
need you
want you
now
and this touching makes us feel
    oh so very real
yes this touching makes us feel
    oh so very real

Karachi was the next destination, where I spent several days trying to secure a visa to travel to Saudi Arabia and trying to subdue an intestinal discomfort that had developed during my stay in Pakistan. Failure at both endeavors brought me to a state of frustration, weakness and dehydration. Everything I consumed was ejected in liquid form at such high pressure that I thought I was developing a new rocket fuel.

Changing my travel plans, I decided to go to Egypt and spend some time in Cairo for rest and rehabilitation before continuing on to Senegal, Côte d'Ivoire, and Kenya.

The trip from Karachi to Cairo turned out to be a real adventure. On a very hot day in May (43°C or 110°F), I made my way to the airport. With two large bags to check the bargaining began. How much was it going to cost me to get my bags out of Pakistan? Bakshesh is an annoying custom that is difficult for the uninitiated, and the most helpful aid I had discovered was a patient and sincere smile. After exchanging some dollars for rupees I paid my final tribute to the economy of Pakistan and made my way to the departure gate. Finding a seat in the departure lounge I tried to relax with some deep breathing exercises, then settled into reading. I had decided to abstain from eating so as not to fuel the conflagration taking place in my bowels, and vowed that my sphincter would not relax until I was in my room at the Ramses Hilton in Cairo.

After four hours of flight delays we were called to board the plane. Having become acclimated to the heat of the terminal, I was still not ready for the oven of the tarmac. We stood in line for forty-five minutes on the black asphalt, the air dancing as the intense heat rose off the tarmac. Children screaming, parents fussing, everyone sweating in the sauna of heat and fumes. Finally the door to the plane was opened and we were allowed to enter the air-conditioned cabin. The temperature change was so great that my body couldn't register a response in the normal manner. It was like walking out of a winter sauna and rolling naked in the snow. An emergency call for blankets and a plea to lighten up on the air conditioning rang out through the plane and we were off to our first stop, Bahrain. Just a short pause in the flight to pick up more passengers—women fresh from the giant duty-free shop, carrying TVs, VCRs, and video cameras, with children in tow, all festooned with gold jewelry. Soon we were in the air once more on our way to Egypt.

In Egypt, as in many countries, foreign nationals arriving without a visa must acquire the proper documents upon entry. This detour added another hour to my journey. I finally made my way to the baggage claim area. The bags were not there yet, so I inquired and was told that they would be coming shortly. Well, I waited another hour before they arrived. So far twelve hours had passed since anything had passed from the internal combustion of my beleaguered bowels. My theory of nothing goes in nothing comes out had worked so far, but I was beginning to feel a marked increase in pressure building up inside me.

I brought my two suitcases to the customs inspection station and presented them to the customs official. He opened both of them and I realized, by their condition, that they had already been very thoroughly scrutinized. The customs inspector spent the next forty-five minutes emptying both cases onto the counter and asking the most inane questions. My patience was wearing thin. The internal pressure was building, and I had reached a point were I was looking forward to a body search, the consequences of which would have plastered the poor unsuspecting inspector to the nearest wall with the sheer unimaginable tsunami of liquid shit that would greet his probing finger. Fortunately for everyone the body search did not take place, but the inspector's actions did send me over the edge. He took all my vitamins and dumped them out on to the counter. Knowing that the Nile Delta has one of the highest concentrations of communicable diseases in the world, I felt the vitamins had been rendered useless. Instantly I reacted, brushing the pills off the counter with such a fury that they were sent flying all over the room. Staring at the inspector I shouted, "May a thousand camels piss on you!" The official stepped back, turned and ran to an office. Immediately I realized I had lost it, and with that realization always comes a mega-dose of humility and insight, could have–should have shit.

A man emerged from the office, tall, in a uniform bedecked with medals, carrying himself with the confidence of much life experience. He looked at me and all my stuff strewn all over the counter. He took my journal from the shoulder bag lying on the counter. Opening the book, he pointed to a photo on the first page and looked at me. My wife I said. Then he pointed to a photo on the inside of the cover, again glancing at me quizzically. My home I answered. He finally spoke and asked why I was carrying so many carpets with me? For my wife and my home I replied. Do you have any children? he asked. With all sincerity I looked into his eyes and said, "Children are a blessing that Allah has not bestowed on me." His smile warmed my heart. He turned to the customs inspector and told him to clean up the mess and pack the suitcases and bring them out to the taxi stand. Walking around the counter, he put his arm around me and said, "Welcome to Egypt." Then, walking me to the taxi stand he called for a limo, wished me a pleasant stay in Cairo, and said something to the driver. After the bags were loaded we were off to the Ramses Hilton. Upon arrival the limo driver wouldn't take any payment from me.

After registering at the hotel desk and giving my bags to the bellman I stopped at the hotel tobacco shop on my way to my room. Twenty years had unfolded since I had fallen in love with Egyptian cigarettes. They were increasingly difficult to find, so I picked up a pack of my favorite brand, coincidentally called Ramses, an oval-shaped ochre-colored cigarette with a taste and feel that had seduced me completely in the sixties. Knowing that I was coming to the end of my smoking days I wanted to revisit the experience. When I arrived in my room I removed my clothes, got the shower to the right temperature, sat on the can, fastened my seat belt, and lit up one of those great smokes. One toot was all it took. My body exploded, and in a nanosecond my bowels were empty. I threw the smokes into the toilet, flushed it, and cleaned myself up in the shower. Transformation—Smoking was gone. It has been my experience that if I can link the pleasure to the pain it becomes much easier to let go of a bad habit. I felt cleansed and walked naked onto the balcony of my room to watch the sun setting behind the Great Pyramids at Giza. Awe, that great vehicle, transported me beyond all concepts.

Eventually, after all this travel and endless and varied negotiations, and the efforts of so many people—chief among them being Ann Farris and Sue Harvey—we were successful in bringing to Vancouver's Expo 86 about two hundred performers from around the world to extol the art of the drum. For two weeks the musicians performed in or outside their home pavilion, or on some of the smaller performance stages that were scattered around the Expo site. Toward the end of the second week 120 of us came together on the main Expo Theatre stage and presented four spectacular concerts that touched us all very deeply.

The World Drum Festival at Expo 86 was the fulfillment of a longtime dream and confirmation of a strong intuitive knowing that changed my life. The whole event was documented by Niv Fichman in a wonderful film titled "World Drums," produced by Rhombus Media with the support of the National Film Board of Canada.

> At Expo 86: "This weekend's finale to the World Drum Festival best validated Expo's rhetoric about international understanding and cooperation. It was, literally, a world in motion, a world in touch...one of those one-of-a-kind memories..."
>
> —Vancouver Sun

With this World Drum Festival began a process of exploring and integrating the drumming traditions of the world into performance experiences that have enriched my life and expanded my understanding of how music can create a more universal sensibility.

At the Winter Olympics (1987): "WORLD DRUMS was not only a breathtaking display of percussion from around the world, it was a communal celebration that captured the true international spirit of the Olympics more than any other art festival event... an exhilarating trip through the most primal and possibly pure form of non-verbal communication."

— CALGARY HERALD

The latest World Drums production brought over three hundred performers together at Expo 2000 in Hannover, Germany, adding many new musicians to the World Drums family. I have much admiration and respect for the skills of producer Karen Kopp who made this event such a success.

Music has been a magic carpet transporting me around the world many times, fostering deep bonds of friendship and demonstrating the wonderful unison and harmony that is part of the human spirit in every culture.

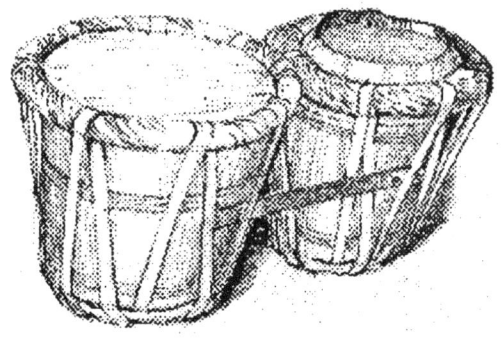

World Drum Guides

The cultural program that supported the Winter Olympics in Calgary provided the opportunity to work with Ed Thigpen, an artist who has been a powerful motivation throughout my life in music. His work with Oscar Peterson had lit a fire in me that burns to this day. At that time I actually didn't know what it was about Ed's music that touched me, but touch me it did and helped guide me over the hurdles faced by a curious young musician. With hindsight and the insight of experience, I think it's Ed's ability to accompany, his example of being the servant of the music, that reached me.

Inspired by the ancient frame drumming traditions of the world, Glen Velez has set an example for all artists, the example of integrity and discipline and the rewards of following your own path and allowing your own curiosity to design your own unique music. Glen's music brings the world together. His evolution of hand drumming techniques and their synthesis with Mongolian harmonic singing has created a captivating sound that has enriched the language of music.

Trichy Sankaran, the great mrdangam master from Madras, India, is simply one of the most powerful musicians I have every worked with. The reverence in this man for his art is palpable. The devotion, power and inspiration of the consummate artist resonates in his music. Place Sankaran on a stage with any number of great musicians and he will kick everyone's butt and they will all love the experience.

In 1988 World Drums created a series of concerts for Expo 88 in Brisbane, Australia, that involved ninety performers from around the world. After this week of events in Brisbane, we formed a smaller ensemble of twenty-five musicians and did a tour of Queensland, traveling north along the Great Barrier Reef all the way to Cairns. In every town a press conference had been organized. Glen, Trichy, Sal and I attended these press conferences, performing and doing interviews with the members of the press. Glen brought his *riqq* (Egyptian tambourine), Trichy had his *kanjira* (South Indian tambourine), Sal had a *berimbau* (Brazil–Capoeira), and I had a pair of shakers. Even with his tiny tambourine Trichy was a tiger with a proficiency and concentration that gave him a lot to say. Usually Glen, Sal and I would settle for playing very simple licks that accompanied Trichy's virtuosic performance.

Upon arriving in the Town of Mackay the four of us were ushered to the press conference that was being held in the glass-walled lobby of the beautiful new concert hall. Trichy began to prepare his kanjira for performance by dampening the skin head so it would loosen up and reach the desired playing condition. But the head of the kanjira had become *too* loose, so Trichy set out to place the instrument in the direct sunlight in order to tighten the head. Unfortunately Trichy didn't notice the glass wall and discovered it quite abruptly. He rebounded and slowly staggered about. The sound of the impact drew a platoon of assistants to help determine the damages. Realizing that Trichy was stunned but okay, Sal suggested to Glen and me that it might be a good time to play some music. Maybe the impact would slow Trichy down enough to allow us to stretch out a little more. It worked. Trichy's notes-per-moment ratio fell dramatically and left a lot of room for us to express ourselves.

Sharda Sahai, head of the Benares Gharana, is a great tabla master from the North Indian Hindustani culture. In World Drums concerts he often joined Sankaran, who represents the Karnatak tradition of South India, in a duet that was always an astonishing musical experience. The challenge with these duets was keeping them within the allotted time so the concerts would be a reasonable length. I always introduced Sharda and Trichy as "These great masters from India." Invariably, their duet would be much longer than I'd planned for the show. When I'd ask Trichy about this he would reply that Sharda controlled the length of their dialogue. When I spoke with Sharda he would tell me that Trichy was in charge of the duration. One evening, in Gladstone, Queensland, their duet was simply cosmic, and everyone was completely blown away. The problem was that their ten-minute spot had lasted twenty-five minutes. I ran back stage to confront them together. Trichy saw the fire in my eyes and quietly said, "I am thinking the masters had a lot to say tonight."

Abraham Kobina Adzenyah—His performance is always a fresh infusion of vitality, confirming once again the positive influence of dance (body motion) on the levels of energy, endurance, and relaxation one can access through music. As a young man Abraham was a member of the Ghana National Dance Ensemble, where he learned and performed the music and dance of the various ethnic traditions of Ghana. Although Abraham comes from the Fanti ethnic group, a part of the great Akan culture, the music I have learned and performed with Abraham comes from the Akan, Ewe, and Dagomba traditions.

Abraham has changed the way I perceive, the way I feel, and the way I perform music. African drumming traditions have helped me look at rhythm from many new perspectives, enriching perception and enhancing enjoyment of all music. For example, take a piece of music based on a twelve-beat rhythmic cycle and explore the variety of ways it can be perceived and felt with conviction. Simple math skills show us that a dance of twelve beats can easily be divided by one, two, three, four, and six, and felt in a very natural way. This variety of perceptions enriches our personal experience of the music and turns a simple phrase into a kaleidoscope of interactions. When Art becomes multidimensional it invites interaction and participation. In our Western-European-based cultures we have placed Art on a pedestal. Museums and concert halls and recordings traditionally limit our perspectives and inhibit participation by all but an elite group of trained specialists. In many cultures in the world, music is a community-based experience, often performed outdoors, and involves the entire population, from children to elders. Seasoned master musicians and dancers guide the community through the experience and the multiplicity of perceptions and different levels of participation, i.e., different rhythmic perspectives, dance, singing, clapping, all combined to offer a rich experience that inspires prolonged involvement, a process that unifies the community and celebrates the family of humanity. Truly a music of the people, by the people, and for the people.

In 1980 Nexus produced an LP called "The Music of NEXUS." The recording included a wide spectrum of music that reflected our current repertoire and included a piece we called "Kobina," dedicated to our friend and mentor, Abraham Kobina Adzenyah. (Kobina actually means Tuesday and refers to Abraham's day name as he was born on a Tuesday.) The music was based on a recreational dance of the Ewe people of southeastern Ghana and Togo called "Gahu." Nexus has never presented the music of other cultures with any assumptions of authenticity, and often we add new and different voices to the music as our imaginations are inspired to participate.

The following year, in 1981, Nexus celebrated its tenth anniversary with a series of three concerts at the St. Lawrence

Centre in Toronto. One of the concerts featured Abraham and the music of Africa. The late seventies and the early eighties were the dawn of the digital recording process and through our co-productions with the CBC we were able to secure good tapes of all three anniversary concerts.

Then in 1982 I received a call from Abraham. He was very upset and told me that we had a major problem to resolve. Apparently his Ewe friends had heard our LP with the recording of "Kobina" and threatened him with violence. According to their cultural tradition at the time, and naively unbeknownst to Nexus, it was against tradition to record and/or receive any commercial gain from their music. They were holding Abraham, as our teacher, responsible for our transgression. A long conversation ensued that touched on the process of teaching and the inability of the mentor to control the use and evolution of insight within the student, on cultural appropriation, and many other ramifications of the incident. I promised Abraham that I would write a letter to his Ewe friends apologizing for our actions and vindicating Abraham of any responsibility in the matter. I sent the letter and also included a copy of our 1981 anniversary concert tape that featured the music of Africa and asked Abraham to play it for his Ewe friends. When I asked Abraham how his friends had reacted to our tape, he smiled and said that they had cried and told him to bring Nexus to Ghana to help them teach their children.

I've shared the stage with many musicians from many different cultures. Most of the artists have been patient advisors as I wander naively along the path of the drum. I've learned so much from all of them and appreciate their artistry and positive spirits.

THE MUSIC OF THE WORLD

From a global perspective, while English is establishing itself as the language of commerce, music has most certainly established itself as the language of the heart. Around the world, performing artists and composers are exploring and sharing the musics of the world in their search to satisfy their curiosity and to fuel their imaginations.

From pop music, musical theater, and contemporary art music, we find the ethnic music of the world's great and diverse cultures answering the artist's call for inspiration. In my travels I have been astonished by the extraordinary variety of human expression that is the voice of the people. The rhythms and colors that people organize in their own unique ways to express their feelings and their observations of daily life offer a perpetual treasury of the face of humanity.

In North America, we live in immigrant cultures and share a wealth of global influences. Unfettered by centuries of tradition, there is greater freedom to explore and develop our own response to these influences.

World music courses and centers have been developed at many schools. Many colleges and universities offer steel pan ensemble, gamelan ensemble, and African drumming ensemble, bringing the arts of the Caribbean, Indonesia, and Africa to post-secondary levels of education in North America. The gamelans of Indonesia represent some of the most sublime evolutions of the art of percussion and the art of ensemble performance in the world. The steel pan is an instrument of the twentieth century, an extraordinary example of recycling. The genius of the people of the Caribbean transformed the castoffs of the oil industry into amazing musical instruments—sources of sound that have enabled the artists of the islands to share the spirit of their culture with the rest of the world.

The drumming ensembles of Africa are as rich and varied as the myriad of cultural traditions that make up the creative treasure house that is Africa. African drumming offers an immediate insight into the strength of simplicity, music as a complete social experience involving the entire community, finding one's place in the ensemble, perceiving rhythms in a variety of ways, drums as melodic instruments and drumming as language (the imitation of the spoken word).

>	Where you find people you will find Music.
>	Experience the vibrations of the family of humanity.

>	For thousands of years, drummers—
>	with their dance of rhythmic gestures—
>	have been celebrating the changes of life
>	from powerful marshaling forces of military drums
>	to the inner search of the monk following his
>		breath in search of peace
>	the rhythms of our life help us to love and hate—to
>		work and play
>	the pulse of the body—the heart—the breath
>	the rhythm of our walk
>	the tempo of our dance
>	all combine as we celebrate life

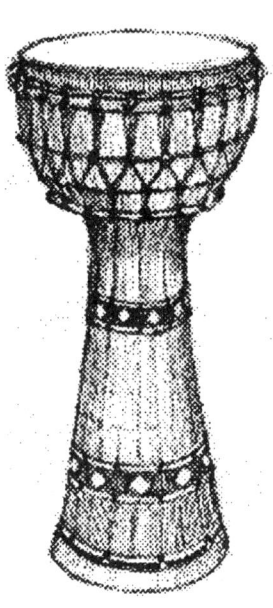

Hand Drumming

We are all involved in the art of touching, using the energy we can access to get things to vibrate. Drums are common to all cultures. But the range of sounds, shapes, and approaches to playing is astounding. The varieties of techniques employed in hand drumming alone could fill many text books. Every culture, every music carries with it another traditional approach to playing that inspires people to sit down and share their ideas. This is one way that artists learn from each other. So musicians sharing their skills is an inspirational experience, a motivational experience, an educational experience. The aesthetics of the cultures of China are influencing the aesthetics of Africa; the aesthetics of Papua New Guinea are influencing the aesthetics of South America. The world is coming together through music.

The great musical traditions of the world are forming a web of intercommunication, touching upon each other and influencing each other in the evolution of the creative spirit of the artists of the world. We are witnessing the evolution of a global music. Technology is most certainly accelerating this process, and I find it a very rich and exciting time.

The human family is joined by music, and drums are at the very heart of it all. From the simple joy of sharing a lick or feeling a groove together, we are drawn into the family of the musical ensemble. As musicians we are blessed with the regular experience of losing ourselves completely in something that is far greater than we are. It is not surprising that hand drumming and drum circles have found their role in music therapy, in groups dedicated to the expansion of consciousness or the development of communication skills, and the simple central task of finding oneself.

An expansion of interest in the art of hand drumming has led to many new opportunities for expression, communication, and the exploration of new cultural influences.

In our search for the roots of the drum, we can travel the ancient pathways of all the cultural traditions of humanity. Eventually we find that the origins of the drum are literally at the very heart of the human condition. The pulse of one's own being is an embryonic perception. The heart of the source—mother—is certainly a powerful pulse in the womb. The rhythms of the heart and the cycles of the breath are the tempo of our lives.

We see in the drumming traditions of the earth a huge motivational resource. Active in the arts of healing, revealing, and appealing, rhythm turns work into dance, physical love into orgasm, and trance into a glance of altered consciousness.

Drumming is dance—energy in motion. Many forms of drumming are an integral part of dance or movement of some sort. The Korean culture has combined drumming and dance into an extraordinary spectacle. Sri Lanka, China, Japan, Africa, the islands of the Caribbean and the Indian Ocean all have traditions of drummers who dance while they are playing. Aboriginal peoples around the world use rhythm and movement to access altered states of consciousness for such functions as healing, dreaming, story telling, etc. Most of the drumming schools or clubs of South America are based on dance forms.

The music of the drum can inspire and direct our actions. Wandering through life, motivated by our natural curiosity and inspired by the creative responses to the challenges of our daily lives, we can stretch out and explore. Once we embark on a course of action, guides will appear along the way to provide direction, motivation and inspiration.

Find a Guide. All cultures have established methods of teaching their traditional arts—schools, private studios of master teachers, or recreational clubs that specialize in local musical traditions, i.e. the pan yards of the Caribbean and the samba clubs of Brazil. Go to the music that turns you on. Go to the performers that inspire you. Great performers are not always great teachers, but if their performance inspires activity on your part, they qualify as guides. The greatest guides don't teach—they share discovery.

Let the drum be your teacher. Your instrument is a school for the imagination. The university of life offers no degrees, but teaches us that learning is the daily evolution of our collective experience. Share your knowledge, build a bridge to a new culture.

One of the major lessons we all have to learn in life is the lesson of simplicity. I remember an experience at a world drum festival where a young performer had his drum kit, as elaborate as could be, with every conceivable kind of rig for drums and cymbals and enough pedals to service an octopus.

After a few rehearsals he approached Trichy Sankaran, who had been playing the mrdangam, and said to him, "I'm sitting here next to you behind the wheel of a Rolls Royce of drum sets with all the bells and whistles, and you're blowing me away with a hollowed out log."

The lesson of simplicity had appeared on the horizon of his life experience.

Nurture your dreams. You are the pilot of your own ship. You can be whatever you can imagine. Find your own way, create your own music, build your own ensembles, study dance or some form of movement, learn to store your songs in your instrument, and sing your heart out.

Music is a universal language. World consciousness is evolving, and although this is challenging many traditions, we are enriched by our differences. Life leads those who will change; those who won't are dragged along bitching and screaming. To embrace change is to accept that life is so much more than we know.

As musicians we must surrender ourselves to the music. We must become a servant of sound. The music, as it unfolds, will direct us and answer all our questions.

Epilogue

Oh Sacred Sound—What I have found
Within Your Care—Within the Ear
The Stillness There—to Be Aware
Of what was always here
You've carried me
from nowhere—to now here

Biblioguides

Anon., *The Way of a Pilgrim*. Trans. R.M.French. London: S.P.C.K., 1960.

Blofeld, John, ed. *The Zen Teachings of Huang Po*. Boston, London: Shambhala, 1958.

Cage, John. *Notations* (with Alison Knowles). New York: Something Else Press, 1969.

____ *A Year from Monday*. Middletown, Conn.: Wesleyan University Press, 1967.

____ *Silence*. Middletown, Conn.: Wesleyan University Press, 1961.

Claxton, Guy. *Hare Brain Tortoise Mind*. London: Fourth Estate, 1998.

Deng Ming-Dao. *Everyday Tao*. Harper Collins, 1996.

____ *Scholar Warrior*. Harper Collins, 1990.

____ *365 Tao*. Harper Collins, 1992.

Emerson, Ralph Waldo — anything.

Gibran, Kahlil. *A Treasury of Kahlil Gibran*, Vols. I & II. New York: Citadel Press, 1962.

Giono, Jean. *The Man Who Planted Trees*. London: The Harvill Press.

Grigg, Ray. *The Tao of Zen*. Boston: Charles E. Tuttle Co., Inc., 1994.

Kapleau, Philip. *The Three Pillars of Zen*. Garden City, New York: Anchor Press/Doubleday, 1980 (1965).

____ *Awakening to Zen*. New York: Scribner, 1997.

Khan, Hazrat Inayat. *Music*. Lahore, Pakistan: Sh.Muhammad Ashraf, 1971.

Lao Tzu. *Tao Te Ching*. Trans. Ursula K. Le Guin. Boston, London: Shambhala, 1998.

Lao Tzu. *Tao Te Ching*. Trans. Stephen Mitchell. Harper Perennial, 1988.

McLuhan, T.C. *Touch The Earth*. Pocket Book Editions, Simon & Schuster, 1971.

_____ *Cathedrals of the Spirit*. Toronto: Harper Collins, 1996.

Osbon, Diane K., ed. *A Joseph Campbell Companion*. New York: Harper Collins, 1991.

Ramanasramam, Sri. *Talks with Sri Ramana Maharshi*, Vol.1-3. Tiruvanmalai.

Richards, Mary Caroline. *Centering*. Wesleyan University Press, 1964.

Rinpoche, Namgyal. *The Womb, Karma, and Transcendence*. Kinmount, Ontario: Bodhi Publishing, 1996.

Rumi, Jelaluddin. *The Essential Rumi*. Trans. Coleman Barks. Harper Collins, 1995.

Schafer, R. Murray. *The Book of Noise*. Arcana Editions, 1998.

_____ *A Sound Education*. Arcana Editions, 1991.

_____ *The Thinking Ear*. Arcana Editions, 1986.

Takemitsu, Toru. *Confronting Silence*. Berkeley, Cal.: Fallen Leaf Press, 1995.